GARDEN *stitch* ✦ LIFE ✦

Garden Stitch Life
First Published in 2018 by Zakka Workshop, a division of World Book Media, LLC
www.zakkaworkshop.com
134 Federal Street
Salem, MA 01970 USA
info@zakkaworkshop.com

AOKI KAZUKO NO STITCH LIFE (NV70342)
Copyright © 2016 Kazuko Aoki/ NIHON VOGUE-SHA.
All rights reserved.
Originally published in Japanese language by NIHON VOGUE Corp.
English language rights, translation & production by World Book Media, LLC
Email: info@worldbookmedia.com

Photographers: Yukari Shirai, Noriaki Moriya, & Kazuko Aoki
English Translation: Ai Toyoda Jirka
English Language Editor: Lindsay Fair

ISBN: 978-1-940552-37-8

Printed in China

10 9 8 7 6 5 4 3 2 1

GARDEN
stitch
LIFE

50 Embroidery Motifs & Projects
to Grow Your Inspiration

KAZUKO AOKI

Introduction

Cup of coffee in hand, I walk through the garden and open the door to my atelier. *What should I start with today?* I select a thread color I had trouble deciding on yesterday, and then I review the design before I get to work stitching. I find that my mind is clear and I'm most productive in the morning.

Throughout the day, I make several trips back and forth between the house and atelier. Each trip involves a walk through my small but beloved garden. The garden doesn't just influence my embroidery style, it also plays a major part in my everyday life.

With this collection of projects, I invite you into my world of embroidery. In addition to floral motifs, you'll find projects inspired by my favorite things, including food, travel, and design. I'll share a bit of my creative process, from inspiration and design to stitching tips and techniques, plus offer a behind-the-scenes look at my studio.

I believe that the best things in life are simple and that every day can be improved with a little stitching!

—Kazuko Aoki

Contents

Part One
In the garden

♥ ♥ ♥

After spending decades devoted to growing roses, I recently made the switch to a low maintenance garden that I can enjoy year-round. During the redesign process, I considered the bees, ladybugs, lizards, and other wildlife and opted to go organic. I also increased the number of deciduous trees and native plants, and made sure to leave plenty of open space for gentle breezes and leisurely strolls. The result is a naturally balanced garden that fits my taste today: simple and mature.

Seed Packet Bag

Use this simple tote to store leftover seeds from last year or new packets you've been collecting for the future. Make sure to add a handle so you can hang the bag in a cool, dry place.

INSTRUCTIONS ON PAGES 66–67

Every fall, I order my flower seeds for the next season. When the time is right, I sow the seeds and then patiently wait for them to sprout before moving them outside. The process is always the same, yet I never tire of it—I am continuously amazed that one tiny seed can grow into a big, beautiful flower and that one small packet of seeds can grow into a whole field of flowers.

Foxglove

Corn Flower

Wild Carrot

WILD FLOWERS
Old Meadow Mixture

Gardener's Patches & Seed Packet

These sweet little patches can be used to decorate a card or embellish a scrapbook. You can even add them to clothing so you can literally wear your love for gardening on your sleeve! Combine embroidery, cotton fabric, and green tulle to create a mixed media seed packet replica.

INSTRUCTIONS ON PAGES 68–71

Violet Notebook

With nearly 500 different species, violets exhibit a wide range of colors and patterns.
These pretty flowers can be seen blooming in the corner of my garden every spring.

INSTRUCTIONS ON PAGES 72–75

Viola tricolor

Sweet violet

Viola arvensis

While visiting England, I came across a tiny yellow viola growing in the brush on the edge of a wheat field. The delicate little flower, known as *Viola arvensis*, was only the size of my pinky fingernail!

Rose Collage

Pink roses have always been my personal favorite, but red, yellow, and orange also make for pretty color combinations. This collage was inspired by my love of all things rose related.

INSTRUCTIONS ON PAGES 76–78

Rose Greeting Cards

Combine embroidered roses, fabric scraps, and vintage stamps to create handmade cards for special occasions. I like to embroider these rose motifs on print fabric to add color and dimension.

INSTRUCTIONS ON PAGE 79

At one time, I had close to 100 rose bushes growing in my small garden. I have so many fond memories associated with roses—the smell of fresh leaves each spring, the site of plump buds, and of course, arranging the blooming flowers into colorful bouquets. Since redesigning my garden, I only have a few rose bushes left, but they continue to bloom every year.

Garden Sampler

Allium christophii, also known as Stars of Persia, are one of my favorite flowers to embroider. These show-stopping flowers have long, graceful stems and large, round heads packed with up to 100 individual metallic purple star-shaped blooms. Believe it or not, these flowers belong to the onion family!

INSTRUCTIONS ON PAGES 83–87

When embroidering a garden scene with a variety of flowers, I like to incorporate different materials to add texture. Tulle provides an excellent foundation for the garden bed, while metal wire adds dimension and contrasts with the softness of the embroidery floss.

Alphabet Sampler

This playful sampler was inspired by a childhood pastime of collecting and arranging twigs to form letters. I used variegated green floss for the leaves to add subtle shading. Incorporating variegated floss into your work will expand your color palette.

INSTRUCTIONS ON PAGE 88

I find that variegated floss can sometimes produce too much color variation, so I will often mix it with solid color floss. The leaves in the Alphabet Sampler were stitched with two strands of solid floss and one strand of variegated floss.

Bee Sampler

I see so many different types of bees while working in my garden. Honeybees, bumblebees, and carpenter bees are easy to identify, but there are many other species that visit too. I find it so interesting to observe the relationship between the bees and flowers. Watching these industrious creatures work makes me love them even more.

INSTRUCTIONS ON PAGES 81–82

Gardening Twine Cannister

Just like hand embroidery, the process of making honey is slow and steady, but extremely rewarding. I embroidered a group of worker bees onto a small hoop and then attached it to a glass jar to create a useful cannister for storing garden twine.

INSTRUCTIONS ON PAGE 80

Spring Flowers Doily

When designing a floral wreath motif, I prefer to work from observation. First, I pick an assortment of flowers, then I arrange them on a plate of water, adding or removing flowers until I am happy with the design. When arranging the flowers, it is important to consider the balance of color, as well as size and shape. Having a model to reference is especially helpful when stitching tricky areas, such as overlapping stems and leaves.

INSTRUCTIONS ON PAGE 89

This motif features pansies, clematis, forget-me-nots, viola, purple mustard, and *Rodgersia podophylla*.

A Letter to Spring

I know that spring is on the way when the warm winds begin to blow and the garden grows a bit greener every day. These gentle harbingers announce the change of seasons as effectively as a letter in the mail. I created my own letter by embellishing white linen with acrylic paint and embroidery, then folding it into an envelope shape. Just add a stamp and it will be fit to send through the mail.

INSTRUCTIONS ON PAGES 90–91

Garden Visitors

When the winter winds blow the leaves from the trees, I make wreaths of in-shell peanuts and leave baskets of bread crusts and tangerines for the birds. My quiet winter garden grows more lively as Japanese white-eyes, Japanese tits, and bulbuls stop by for a snack.

INSTRUCTIONS ON PAGES 92–93

Bird Studies

Robins and fieldfares are two of my favorite birds; unfortunately, I don't see too many of them in my garden. Attach a wire to these embroidered avians for a pretty decoration, or add a pin to the back to create a brooch.

INSTRUCTIONS ON PAGE 94

Fall Field Samples

Mushrooms occasionally make an appearance in my garden. I'm always hoping to see a fly amanita mushroom with its iconic red cap with white spots. After embroidering this classic mushroom motif, I made it into a brooch—it's almost as good as the real thing!

INSTRUCTIONS ON PAGES 96–97

I love collecting acorns, leaves, and other treasures during autumn walks through the neighborhood. I find that I notice so many more oak trees once the acorns start to fall to the ground!

Acorn Knitting Needles

This design was inspired by a pair of knitting needles made with real acorns. These needles feature acorns made from wool felt, allowing them to be lightweight and easy to use.

INSTRUCTIONS ON PAGE 95

Chamomile Sachet
& Foldover Clutch

These simple bags are perfect
for travel —use them to store
toiletries and small supplies.
I always like to pack few empty
bags for collecting herbs
and other plant clippings
on my travels.

INSTRUCTIONS ON
PAGES 98–101

Herb Patches

Embroider herb patches to customize slippers for a spa-like experience at home. This design features common rue, which is known for its oblong leaves.

INSTRUCTIONS ON PAGE 108

Inspiration: My Garden

I have a small garden between my house and atelier; but to me, it's just the right size. My garden is the result of lots of trial and error: deciding where to plant each flower, experimenting with different seeding techniques, and working to make each flower bloom.

When I find myself in need of a break from embroidery, I head out to the garden. As soon as I'm outside, I think of a million tasks to be done: trimming branches, cleaning out beds, or planting an empty area. No matter how much I accomplish, it always seems like there's more work to be done.

I never tire of stitching fields of green.

It's fascinating to observe the stages of growth—an entire viola is contained in just one tiny seed!

This label is one of my all-time favorite shades of green. When I feel lost, I always start from this color.

After years of use, these FELCO pruning shears fit my hands perfectly. Plus, they cut branches like butter.

Greenery grows quickly and often needs to be pruned. The clippings are perfect for making holiday wreaths.

I have a juneberry tree right outside my atelier. The berries make a tasty jam.

After painting a new motif, I pull out swatches of embroidery floss to find the perfect color match.

In the winter, I cut up pieces of bread crust and leave them out for the birds. I think it's funny that the birds are dining on the same bread as my family!

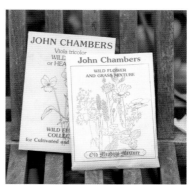

I like to buy seed packets as souvenirs while traveling. Wildflowers grew from these British seeds.

This snapshot features a few seedlings, including white lace flower, violet cress, and valerian.

I make my own potting soil from a blend of akadama red ball earth, leaf compost, and rice husk charcoal.

Another souvenir from England: jute twine. It's the perfect size to carry in your pocket while working in the garden.

This is a selection of green embroidery floss and yarn inspired by the plants of England.

My completed Christmas wreath—it comes together quickly if you use a wreath base.

I start planning which threads to use while I am painting.

Having fresh flowers in the house makes me happy. Creating arrangements from things I've grown in my own garden has inspired me to use plants in unexpected ways. I find myself incorporating greenery, fruit, and other parts of the plant that are often overlooked.

When redesigning my garden, I made sure to incorporate plants with dark flowers and foliage, as well as ones with light, silvery leaves. These plants provide contrast to the sea of green and all the pastel colored flowers. In turn, I've begun incorporating darker colors into my embroidery for added depth.

Rosebuds are one of my favorite motifs to embroider.

I love the smell of the flowers when the kumquat tree blooms in July, but I love the taste of kumquat jam even more!

I ordered this rose from Peter Beales Roses. It has a beautiful, powerful fragrance.

I have a few fruit bushes growing in the backyard.

Allium flowers bloom in an incredibly unique ball shape. Every year, I find myself marveling at their natural construction.

Removing kumquat seeds is a time-consuming process, but the jam is so delicious that it is worth the work.

Commonly known as forget-me-nots, myosotis bloom every year.

These purple Japanese asters, known as kongiku in Japan, are one of my favorite flowers. I discovered them on a walk and had to grow them in my garden.

Chinese hound's tongue are very similar to forget-me-nots, but exhibit a different shade of blue.

Roses climb over the roof of my bicycle shed. They bloom in spring and produce lots of red hips in the fall.

Helleborus, black ball cornflower, and royal purple smoketree add rich purple shades to my garden.

A lit candle, a cross-shaped financier cake, and a bundle of rose hips create a cozy autumn scene.

My garden includes a small pond that is home to a school of Japanese rice fish. The dragonflies also breed here at the beginning of summer.

Deep purple viola grow next to yellow-leaved creeping Jenny.

Velvety lamb's ear leaves always bring a smile to my face. I love the soft feel and silvery green shade of these leaves.

Part Two
Everyday Life

♥ ♥ ♥

I wake up early in the summer, but as the weather changes and the sunrise grows later and later, I allow myself to sleep in a bit more. Regardless of what time I wake, breakfast is always the same: bread with homemade jam, a sunny-side up egg with vegetables, yogurt, seasonal fruit, and tea.

After breakfast, I do a little housework and drink coffee before heading to my atelier. Once the afternoon rolls around, I find the garden calling my name. I'll water and do some planting before running to the grocery store and preparing dinner. I don't embroider at night, so I'll watch television or read.

I occasionally travel or go out in the city, but most of my days follow this routine. I find that having a routine allows me to focus while I'm working in my atelier and tap into my creativity.

Pottery Placemat

Stitch a series of simple bowls, cups, and plates onto a linen place-mat for an elegant upgrade to your table. A black backstitched outline adds a special touch. I use white Teema dishes, designed by Kaj Franck, as my everyday tableware. The minimalist color and shape of this Scandinavian design makes any food you put on them look even better!

INSTRUCTIONS ON PAGES 102–103

Market Bag

I used a supermarket bag as a pattern to draft my own reusable tote. The combination of natural linen and black piping provides a clean, modern look.

INSTRUCTIONS ON
PAGES 104–105

Tobe Ware Sampler

I used a reverse appliqué technique to add dimension and texture to this tobe ware sampler. The kurawanka bowl featured at the top center was always my daughter's favorite dish.

INSTRUCTIONS ON PAGES 106–107

As a teenager, I studied the Japanese folk craft movement and decided that I would use tobe ware for my dishes as an adult. Tobe ware is white porcelain pottery hand painted with indigo designs. Over the years, I have collected some beautiful pieces of tobe ware and use them every day—their simplicity works well with my favorite white dishes.

Bread Magnets

When designing these motifs, I carefully considered which stitches to use in order to capture the texture of bread. Adhere magnets to the wrong side of these patches to add a whimsical touch to your refrigerator.

INSTRUCTIONS ON PAGE 109

In my opinion, starting your day off with freshly baked bread makes any morning better. A new bakery opened in my neighborhood, so I've been sampling all their offerings. I love their sourdough bread and sometimes treat myself to a loaf with fruit and nuts.

Linen Bread Cloth

I like to serve fresh bread in a cloth to keep it warm and soft. If you plan to wash your bread cloth frequently, use short stitches to increase durability.

INSTRUCTIONS ON PAGE 108

Recipe Case

Use this little pouch to store recipe cards. The round leather closure was inspired by an old-fashioned button and string envelope.

INSTRUCTIONS ON PAGES 110–111

When making gifts, I opt for designs that work up quickly and are relatively simple. I want the recipients to enjoy using their gifts every day, rather than saving them for special occasions.

Monogrammed Oven Mitts

I once received an oven mitt as a souvenir from a friend's travels. I loved the idea so much that I came up with my own pattern. If you plan to embroider your oven mitt with cross-stitch, look for a plain-woven linen fabric with nice texture.

INSTRUCTIONS ON PAGES 112–113

Inspiration: My Atelier

I built my atelier, or studio, more than 30 years ago to house a large loom that I brought back from Sweden. The atelier is situated right next to my house and has a large southeast-facing window that lets in a lot of natural light. The design of the studio is quite simple—I work at a desk by the window and store all of my supplies in a closet on the opposite wall.

When the weather is nice, I throw the doors and windows of the atelier open wide. I love being able to smell the roses and hear the bees buzzing around the European privet flowers as I work. Sometimes, a butterfly or dragonfly will fly inside the atelier, which makes me feel like I am at one with nature.

I sometimes cut templates to assist with fabric selection or look at a design from a different point of view.

I love using linen thread to add contrast and dimension to my embroidery.

After much deliberation, I'll use the template to cut the design out of fabric.

There are so many different shades of red. I collect swatches of red ribbon and fabric to help with color selection.

I like to create charts to keep track of which thread colors I used for each design.

The magnificent purple Cardinal de Richelieu rose is the reason I first started embroidering roses.

When traveling, I often bring along an illustrated field guide and jot down the date and location whenever I observe a plant in the wild.

I used these thread swatches to select shades of brown for embroidering bread motifs.

Like many other embroiderers, I collect tools of the trade and always have my eyes peeled for an interesting pair of scissors or pin cushion.

This design was inspired by a geranium I saw in the United Kingdom.

For me, sketching is an important part of the design process.

I collect field guides and often refer to the images when designing new motifs.

When brainstorming a new design, I often create little mood boards within a notebook.

During rose season, I open the door of the atelier to bring the garden inside.

This picture book belonged to my children. The pages are filled with doodles and the spine is taped together, but I still find it quite useful.

Over the years, I've accumulated quite a collection of craft supplies and reference books. I like to spread all of my supplies, books, and notes out on a big table so everything is right in front of me while I work.

Between the flower arrangements, sketches, and embroidery, I can barely see the surface of my desk some days! The nice thing about having a dedicated studio space is not having to stop and clean up when you're in the middle of a project. When I am completely finished with a project, I always make an effort to clean up my workspace because it leaves me feeling refreshed and inspired to start a new project.

My favorite reference books contain both illustrations and photographs.

I use a lot of No. 25 embroidery floss, so I have a special organizer just for this thread.

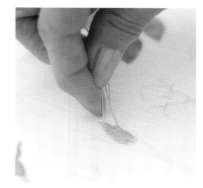

I love to work by the natural light that shines through my studio windows.

I keep a notebook full of mini collages with inspiring color combinations, sketches, and fabrics to consider to future designs.

When designing, I try to remember to keep it simple and will often repeat the same motif.

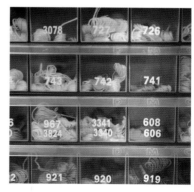

Another view of my No. 25 embroidery floss collection—I have a case with numbered compartments for each shade of thread, organized by color.

My sweet rescue cat enjoys spending time in my atelier too! She loves to nap right on top of my designs.

I like to keep a simple one-color project on hand that I can work on without thinking. I call this my "embroidery medicine."

I also keep color-coordinated boxes of unique fibers and thread scraps. This "thread swamp" is the contents of my green box.

After working at the same desk for many years, the edges are starting to show some wear.

I use these spools of Swedish linen thread for weaving, but I sometimes use them in embroidery too.

I pin inspirational images and personal mementos to a bulletin board in my studio.

I keep weaving materials and other fibers in baskets organized by color or type of thread.

My house and atelier are right next to each other, but sometimes it takes me a while to the leave the house and get to work.

I'll use these fall garden clippings arranged on a plate of water as a model for a sketch.

Part Three
Travels Abroad

♥ ♥ ♥

I studied textiles in Borås, a Swedish
city about four hours from Stockholm
by train. While at school, I worked with
various materials, including cotton, linen,
and wool, and learned about spinning,
knitting, weaving, and printing fabric. It is
so amazing to make a piece of fabric from
start to finish.

School days were always busy, but I fondly
remember taking tea breaks with my fellow
students. We'd often knit while enjoying
a cup of coffee and a slice of cake that
someone had made.

As a result of my time spent in Sweden,
I have a soft spot for Scandinavian design
and my work is greatly influenced by its
simplicity and beauty.

Dala Horse Wall Hangings

In the Dalarna province of Sweden, there is a textile studio called Jobs Handtryck known for its hand-printed fabrics featuring colorful floral designs. I used some scraps from my fabric stash to create these collage-style wall hangings featuring another popular Swedish motif, the Dala horse.

INSTRUCTIONS ON PAGES 114–115

Fussy cut the fabric to create unique patterns within the horse silhouette. An embroidery floss tassel makes for the perfect tail.

Swedish Wildflower Sampler

In Småland, south of Stockholm, there is a community of glass workshops known as "The Kingdom of Crystal." While visiting there, I purchased a glass dish from Kosta Boda that I still love to use to this day. From the company's Ulla collection, the dish features wildflowers and butterflies carved in relief. After researching the different varieties in an illustrated field guide, I've been embroidering these flowers ever since.

INSTRUCTIONS ON PAGES 116–117

Midsummer Tea Cozy

By mid-June, all of Sweden is in bloom and the sun shines almost 24 hours a day. Known as Midsummer, this time is a cause for great celebration. Because the summer season is so short in Sweden, people like to spend as much time as possible outdoors and often enjoy their tea outside.

INSTRUCTIONS ON PAGES 118–119

Sketchbook Studies

Create embroidered sketches to commemorate special trips or events. Once the embroidery is complete, use a hole punch along the top edge to make it look like the page was torn from a sketchbook.

INSTRUCTIONS ON PAGES 120–121

This motif was inspired by a visit to a friend's house in Halmstad, a town on the west coast of Sweden. Along the way, we stopped by the roadside to pick yellow wildflowers. We used this simple arrangement to decorate the dining room table during our stay.

This porcelain teacup was the first thing I bought for my dorm while studying abroad in Sweden. I can clearly remember the housemother warning me to be careful with the fragile handle as I drank my tea in the kitchen. Back in Japan a few years later, the handle broke off while I was washing the cup. This made me remember my housemother with a smile.

ÄPPLE

On my walk to school, I would pass a factory with a garden full of apple trees. On fall evenings, my roommate and I would collect apples that had fallen to the ground and bring them back to our dorm to make Swedish apple cake. I learned a great deal of the Swedish language by searching for recipes. On windy fall days, I always think of those trees and wonder if they're still dropping their apples.

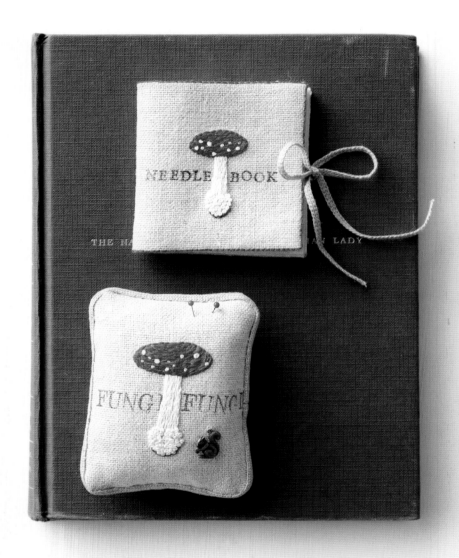

Mushroom Needlebook & Pin Cushion

Mushrooms come in so many amazing shapes and colors, but my favorites are the classic red and white variety, known as fly amanita. Use these whimsical motifs to embellish a needlebook or pin cushion.

INSTRUCTIONS ON PAGES 122–125

Before You Begin

Garden Bees

1
3
2
5
4

Foxglove

Tools & Materials

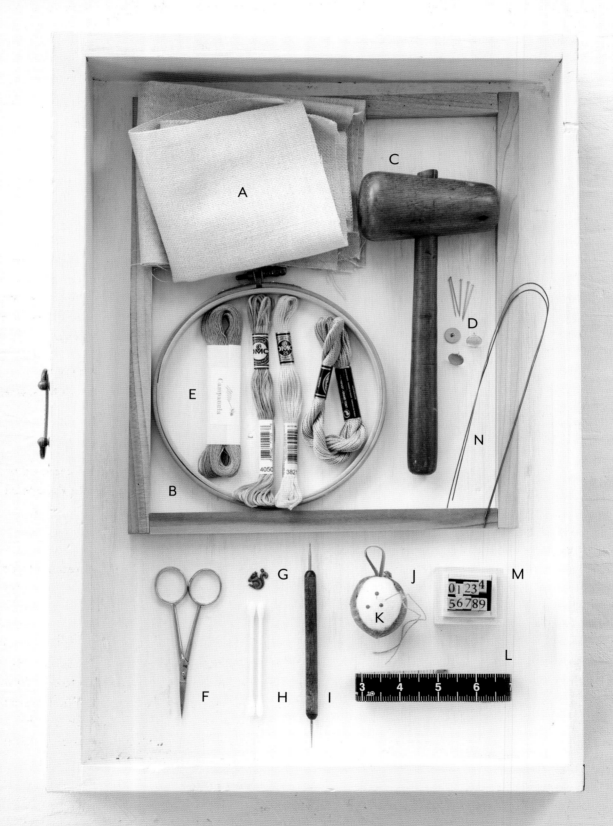

A. FABRIC

I prefer to embroider on linen or linen blend fabric. If using a linen blend, look for a fabric that is around 50% linen and 50% cotton. With most of the projects in this book, you'll be instructed to adhere mid-weight fusible interfacing to the wrong side of the fabric before stitching to add support and stability to the work.

B. HOOPS & FRAMES

I use circular embroidery hoops for small projects and a rectangular frame for large projects. Make sure to select the proper hoop or frame based on the size of your embroidery.

C. WOODEN MALLET

This tool is helpful for securing the pins or tacks when setting embroidery fabric onto a frame or when framing finished embroidery work.

D. PINS & TACKS

Use thumb tacks to secure fabric to a wooden embroidery frame prior to stitching. Thumb tacks and pins can also be used when mounting finished embroidery work onto foam core board. If using pins, look for short, straight pins made of stainless steel, which are often called lace pins.

E. EMBROIDERY FLOSS

DMC No. 25 embroidery floss is used for the majority of projects in this book. DMC Pearl Cotton No. 5 is occasionally used for plant stems, while linen thread is sometimes used to provide contrast and texture.

F. SCISSORS

Use a pair of small, sharp scissors to snip threads and a larger pair to cut fabric.

G. CHARMS

Embellish your work with metal charms to add texture and dimension.

H. COTTON SWABS

Wet the end of a cotton swab, then use it to erase stray marks from transferring the embroidery motif or to tidy up unruly stitches.

I. TRACER

Use a special tracer tool and carbon chalk paper to transfer the embroidery motif onto fabric.

J. EMBROIDERY NEEDLES

Use the appropriate needle size based on the number of strands of floss.

K. SEWING PINS

I recommend using silk pins to hold appliqué fabrics, ribbon, or any other materials in place while working. Silk pins feature thin bodies and small heads, so they won't leave marks on the fabric or get in the way while sewing.

L. MEASURING TAPE OR RULER

Use to check the size of your embroidery or to mark finishing and cutting lines.

M. RUBBER STAMPS

Stamp fabric for a customized, mixed media effect. Just make sure to use ink that's suitable for fabric.

N. WIRE

Add wire to your embroidery to create a three-dimensional effect.

OTHER TOOLS & MATERIALS

You may need additional tools and materials to transfer the embroidery motifs onto your fabric. Carbon chalk paper and tracing paper were used to transfer the projects in this book, but there are a variety of transfer products on the market today, so use the method that works best for you.

Tips & Techniques

The projects in this book are made with basic embroidery stitches. However, I've incorporated some unique techniques, such as rubber stamping, appliqué, and ribbon embroidery, to add texture and dimension to the designs. The following guide includes step-by-step instructions for these special techniques.

RIBBON EMBROIDERY

1. Thread a needle with a 24 in (60 cm) long piece of ribbon. Insert the needle through the short ribbon tail.

2. This will secure the end and prevent the needle from becoming unthreaded.

3. Make a knot at the other end of the ribbon. Insert the needle through the fabric from the wrong side. Thread another needle with a strand of No. 25 embroidery floss in a coordinating color. Insert this needle through the fabric from the wrong side and draw it out right next to the ribbon. Use this floss to running stitch along the center of the ribbon for 20 in (50 cm).

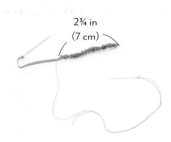

4. Pull the No. 25 embroidery floss to gather the stitched ribbon to 2¾ in (7 cm).

5. Arrange the gathered ribbon into a spiral, adjusting the gathers and pinning in place as you coil.

6. Use the No. 25 embroidery floss to tack down the coiled ribbon in several spots. Bring both the ribbon and floss to the wrong side of the work and finish off.

WORKING WITH VARIEGATED THREAD

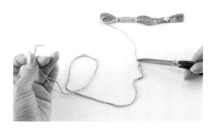

1. Cut a 20-24 in (50-60 cm) long piece of variegated embroidery floss.

2. Cut an equally sized piece of solid embroidery floss. Separate the desired number of strands from each piece of floss. Join the separated strands together to create a mixed piece.

3. Thread the mixed floss onto a needle and start stitching. This photo shows two solid strands combined with one variegated strand, which will create more subtle shading than if using 100% variegated floss.

FUSSY CUTTING FOR APPLIQUÉ

4. This photo shows the various results that can be achieved by working with variegated and solid embroidery floss. From top to bottom: 3 variegated, 2 variegated + 1 solid, 1 variegated + 2 solid, and 3 solid.

1. To help decide which area of the fabric to cut, make a stencil by cutting out the actual appliqué template. Once you've made your selection, apply paper-backed fusible web to the general area on the wrong side of the appliqué fabric.

2. Use a heat erasable marking pen to trace the actual appliqué template onto the appliqué fabric. If using dark appliqué fabric, use a white pen.

3. Cut the fabric out along the marked line.

4. Remove the paper backing from the appliqué motif and adhere it to the background fabric. Make sure to cover the fabric with a piece of parchment paper or a pressing cloth to prevent any glue from sticking to your iron.

5. Backstitch around the outline of the appliqué motif using a coordinating color of thread. Note: The raw edge of the appliqué fabric is still exposed with this method.

RUBBER STAMPING ON FABRIC & APPLIQUÉ

1. Lay the stamp on a flat surface and gently tap the ink pad onto the stamp until it is evenly coated. Make sure to use ink that is suitable for fabric.

2. Firmly press the stamp to transfer the ink to the appliqué fabric.

3. Completed view of the stamped fabric. To appliqué this stamped fabric, you'll need to adhere paper-backed fusible web to the wrong side.

4. Use a pencil to trace the appliqué motif from the book onto tracing paper. Flip the traced image over transfer the reversed motif* onto the wrong side of the appliqué fabric by tracing over the design with a tracer tool (the pressure of the tracer tool will transfer the pencil lines to the fabric). Cut the fabric out along the marked lines.

5. In the following steps, you'll be adhering the appliqué motif to your background fabric and adding embroidery. You can use carbon chalk paper to transfer the embroidery motif, but if your background fabric has a rough texture, you may have some difficulty. Instead, trace the embroidery motif onto freezer paper.

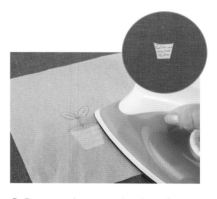

6. Remove the paper backing from the appliqué motif and adhere it to the background fabric. Embroider along the carbon chalk paper lines, or complete the following steps if using freezer paper: First, align the freezer paper on top of the fabric and iron to temporarily secure in place.

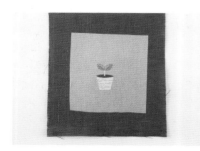

7. Next, embroider the motif, stitching through the freezer paper.

8. Once the embroidery is complete, tear away the freezer paper.

9. Use a needle or seam ripper to remove any remaining bits of paper.

*Note: Transferring the mirror image of the motif will ensure that the finished appliqué appears correctly.

REVERSE APPLIQUÉ

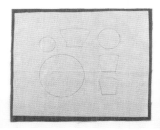

1. Adhere paper-backed fusible web to the wrong side of the main (top) fabric. Transfer the mirror image of the appliqué motif outline to the fusible web.

2. Cut out along the marked lines.

3. Adhere fusible interfacing to the wrong side of the appliqué (bottom) fabric. Transfer the appliqué motif outlines to the right side of the fabric.

4. Remove the paper backing from the main fabric from step 1.

5. Align the main fabric on top of the appliqué fabric, matching up the cutouts with the traced outlines. Press to adhere the two layers together. Use a piece of parchment paper or a pressing cloth to protect your iron.

6. Trace the embroidery motif from the book onto tracing paper. Align the tracing paper on top of the fabric and pin in place.

7. Insert a piece of carbon chalk paper underneath the tracing paper with the chalk side against the fabric. I like to position a sheet of cellophane on top of the tracing paper to make the transfer process smoother. Use a tracer tool to trace over the design. The pressure from the tracing tool will transfer the chalk outline onto the fabric.

8. Use thumb tacks to mount the fabric onto a wooden embroidery frame.

9. Couching stitch around the outline of the appliqué motif, then embroider the rest of the design as noted in the individual project instructions.

HOW TO MAKE A PATCH

1. Adhere fusible interfacing to the wrong side of the fabric and embroider as noted in the individual project instructions.

2. Cut out the embroidered design, leaving a ⅜ in (8 mm) margin. If you leave less fabric, it will be difficult to finish the edges. If you leave more fabric, it will be too bulky.

3. Cut small notches into the margin along the curved areas. Be careful not to cut the embroidery—stop cutting just at the edge of the thread.

4. Completed view of the clipped margin.

5. Use a toothpick to apply glue to the wrong side of the margin. Fold the margin back and adhere it to the wrong side of the embroidery. Periodically check the right side as you work to make sure the margin is folded in the correct place.

6. Cut a piece of felt in the size and shape as the finished embroidery.

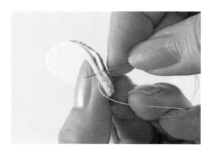

7. Align the embroidery on top of the felt, making sure that the felt is not visible from the front. Whipstitch the embroidery to felt using a coordinating color of thread.

8. Completed view of the felt-backed patch. If desired, sew a brooch pin to the felt backing.

HOW TO MAKE A FELTED ACORN

1. Roll the wool roving into a ball. Form it into an acorn shape by repeatedly stabbing it with a felting needle.

2. It may help to occasionally roll the ball between your fingers to mat the fibers together.

3. Once you've achieved the desired shape, use a knitting needle to poke a hole through the center of the acorn.

4. Insert a threaded needle through the bottom hole and draw it out of the top hole. Pull the thread to hide the tail inside the acorn.

5. Begin buttonhole stitching around the top hole of the acorn in a circle.

6. Continue stitching the acorn cap with spiral rows of buttonhole stitch.

7. Once the embroidery is complete, insert the needle through the top hole and draw it out on the side of the acorn. Pull the thread taut and cut to hide the end inside the acorn.

HOW TO INSTALL EYELETS

1. Align your fabric on top of a hard surface, such as a wood block. Use a punch tool and mallet to make a hole in the fabric at the desired eyelet location. If you don't have a punch tool, use sharp scissors to carefully poke a hole in the fabric.

2. Insert the eyelet shank through the hole from the wrong side of the fabric. If making a button closure, such as the one used in the Recipe Case on page 40, align a leather button on top.

3. Position the eyelet washer on top. Use a setting tool and mallet to hammer the eyelet components together.

HOW TO HEM FABRIC EDGES WITH MITERED CORNERS

 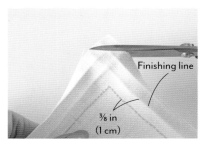 

Finishing line

⅜ in (1 cm)

4. Completed view of an eyelet with a leather button.

1. Backstitch around the edge of the fabric ⅜ in (1 cm) in from the finishing line. Fold the seam allowance in twice and press to mark creases. Unfold and trim the corners at an angle.

2. Fold each corner in, then fold the seam allowance in twice and pin in place.

  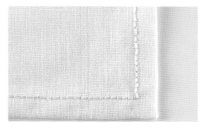

3. Blind stitch the hem by stitching through the folded seam allowance and under the backstitches from step 1.

4. When you reach the corner, sew the mitered corner folds together, then continue sewing along the next side.

5. Completed view of the finished work from the right side. The backstitching serves as a decorative accent.

Project Instructions

♥ ♥ ♥

Before you get started stitching, please take a minute to read through the following notes. This general information applies to all the projects in this book.

- All of the motifs and templates in this book appear at 100% actual size. A couple of the larger motifs have been divided into two pieces in order to fit within the book. When transferring the design to fabric, overlap the two pieces as noted, then trace the complete motif.

- The word "stitch" has been omitted from the diagrams in order to save space. For example, satin stitch simply appears as "Satin."

- DMC No. 25 embroidery floss is used unless otherwise noted. DMC color codes are represented by the three and four digit numbers that appear after the stitch names. You'll also see a note listing the number of floss strands used to make each stitch.

- DMC Pearl Cotton No. 5 and No.8 and linen thread are also used occasionally. I prefer to use my own brand of linen thread, called Kazuko Aoki Original Linen Embroidery Thread, as well as Art Fiber Endo linen thread. There are many other wonderful brands of linen embroidery thread on the market, so I simply provide the general color name, such as green. I generally use one strand of

thread if stitching with anything other than DMC No. 25 embroidery floss.

- Make French knots with one wrap unless otherwise noted. However, the size of your French knots will change based on the number of wraps and how tightly you pull the thread, so adjust according to your personal style if necessary.

- The amount of fabric listed in the materials section of each project represents the bare minimum you'll need. It can be difficult to embroider small pieces of fabric, so I recommend preparing a larger piece of fabric, then trimming it down to size once the embroidery is complete.

- Unless you're embroidering sheer fabric, I recommend adhering mid-weight fusible interfacing to the wrong side of your fabric before embroidering. This will provide stability and support while stitching and help hide messy threads from the wrong side of the work.

Seed Packet Bag

SHOWN ON PAGE 8

MATERIALS

- → DMC No. 25 embroidery floss in 772, 907, and 3772
- → 7½ × 17¼ in (19 × 44 cm) of green linen fabric
- → 9 × 15 in (23 × 38 cm) of cotton fabric (for lining)
- → 1½ × 2 in (4 × 5 cm) of beige cotton fabric (for appliqué)
- → 7½ × 17¼ in (19 × 44 cm) of mid-weight fusible interfacing
- → 1½ × 2 in (4 × 5 cm) of paper-backed fusible web
- → 20 in (50 cm) of ¼ in (5 mm) wide tan leather tape
- → ⅜ in (1 cm) diameter circle of hook and loop tape
- → Script text rubber stamp
- → Sepia ink pad (suitable for use on fabric)
- → Freezer paper

INSTRUCTIONS

1. Adhere fusible interfacing to the wrong side of the green linen fabric.

2. Use the technique shown on page 60 to make the stamped fabric pot and adhere it to the green linen fabric using paper-backed fusible web (refer to the step 4 diagram below for placement). Topstitch the pot to secure the appliqué.

3. Embroider the motif as noted in the diagram at left. If it's too difficult to transfer the embroidery motif onto the fabric due to the rough texture of the linen, try using a sheet of freezer paper as shown on page 60.

4. Once the embroidery is complete, trim the green linen fabric into shape as shown below. This will be the bag outside.

MOTIF (shown at 100%)

- → Use 3 strands unless otherwise noted.

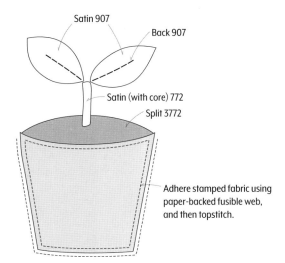

Satin 907

Back 907

Satin (with core) 772

Split 3772

Adhere stamped fabric using paper-backed fusible web, and then topstitch.

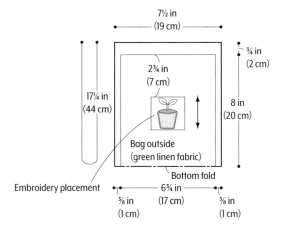

7½ in (19 cm)

¾ in (2 cm)

2¾ in (7 cm)

17¼ in (44 cm)

8 in (20 cm)

Bag outside (green linen fabric)

Embroidery placement

Bottom fold

6¾ in (17 cm)

⅜ in (1 cm)

⅜ in (1 cm)

5. Fold the bag outside in half with right sides together. Sew together along the sides using ⅜ in (1 cm) seam allowance.

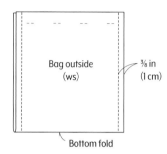

Bag outside (ws)

⅜ in (1 cm)

Bottom fold

6. Cut two 7½ × 9 in (19 × 23 cm) rectangles of cotton fabric for the lining.

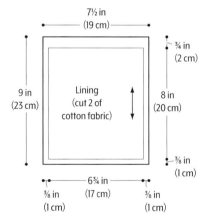

7½ in (19 cm)

9 in (23 cm)

Lining (cut 2 of cotton fabric)

¾ in (2 cm)

8 in (20 cm)

⅜ in (1 cm)

6¾ in (17 cm)

⅜ in (1 cm)

⅜ in (1 cm)

7. Align the two lining pieces with right sides together. Using ⅜ in (1 cm) seam allowance, sew together along the sides and bottom, leaving a 4 in (10 cm) opening at the bottom.

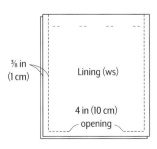

⅜ in (1 cm)

Lining (ws)

4 in (10 cm) opening

8. Press the side seams open on both the lining and bag outside. With right sides together, insert the lining into the bag outside. Cut the leather tape into two 10 in (25 cm) long handles. Sandwich the handles between the bag outside and lining, following the placement noted below. Sew around the top using ¾ in (2 cm) seam allowance.

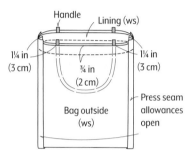

Handle   Lining (ws)

1¼ in (3 cm)

¾ in (2 cm)

1¼ in (3 cm)

Press seam allowances open

Bag outside (ws)

9. Turn the bag right side out through the opening in the lining. Hand stitch the opening closed. Sew the hook and loop tape circles to the lining at the center front and center back of the bag.

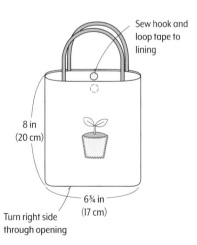

Sew hook and loop tape to lining

8 in (20 cm)

6¾ in (17 cm)

Turn right side through opening

Gardener's Patches

SHOWN ON PAGE 9

MATERIALS

- DMC No. 25 embroidery floss in ECRU, 168, 169, 327, 407, 435, 729, 822, 841, 844, 939, 989, 3078, 3345, 3346, 3348, 3772, 3820, 3821, and 3822
- DMC Pearl Cotton No. 8 in ECRU
- Linen thread in beige
- 8 × 12 in (20 × 30 cm) of white cotton sateen fabric
- 8 × 12 in (20 × 30 cm) of mid-weight fusible interfacing
- 1¼ × 2 in (3 × 5 cm) of text print fabric (or make your own as shown on page 60)
- 1¼ × 2 in (3 × 5 cm) of paper-backed fusible web
- ⅜ × 2½ in (1 × 6 cm) each of blue, pink, and yellow linen fabric
- Alphabet rubber stamps
- Sepia ink pad (suitable for use on fabric)
- ⅜ × ⅝ in (1 × 1.5 cm) lead tape (used for taping golf clubs)
- Craft glue

INSTRUCTIONS

1. Adhere fusible interfacing to the wrong side of the white cotton sateen fabric.
2. Embroider the motifs as noted in the diagrams below and on page 69.
3. Use a toothpick to outline the motifs with craft glue, applying the glue to the white cotton sateen fabric about ¹⁄₁₆ in (2 mm) away from the embroidery.
4. Once the glue is dry, cut the motifs out just beyond the glue outline.
5. If desired, use the rubber stamps to label the blue, pink, and yellow linen fabric with plant names. Trim one end of each label into a point (refer to the photo on page 9 for reference).

MOTIFS (shown at 100%)

- Use 3 strands unless otherwise noted.
- Use No. 25 embroidery floss unless otherwise noted.

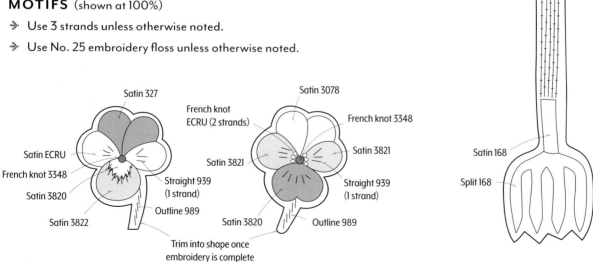

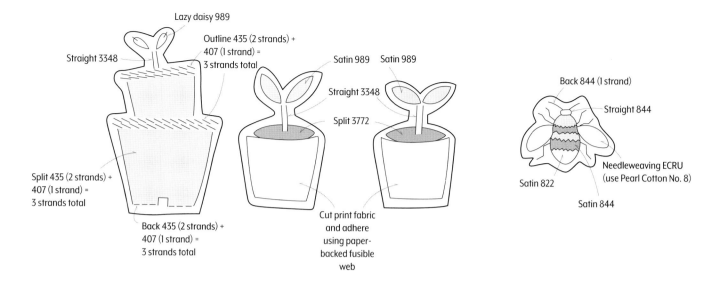

Lazy daisy 989

Outline 435 (2 strands) + 407 (1 strand) = 3 strands total

Straight 3348

Satin 989   Satin 989

Straight 3348

Split 3772

Split 435 (2 strands) + 407 (1 strand) = 3 strands total

Back 435 (2 strands) + 407 (1 strand) = 3 strands total

Cut print fabric and adhere using paper-backed fusible web

Back 844 (1 strand)

Straight 844

Needleweaving ECRU (use Pearl Cotton No. 8)

Satin 822

Satin 844

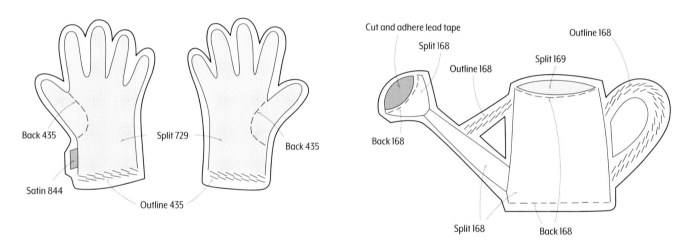

Back 435

Split 729

Back 435

Satin 844

Outline 435

Cut and adhere lead tape

Split 168

Outline 168

Outline 168

Split 169

Outline 168

Back 168

Split 168

Back 168

Make groups of two long vertical straight stitches, then work short horizontal straight stitches on top as shown below

3772 (2 strands) + 435 (1 strand) = 3 strands total

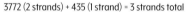

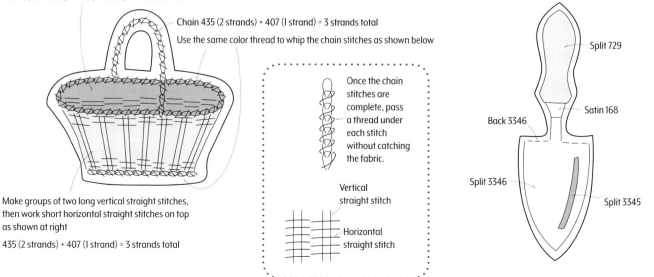

Chain 435 (2 strands) + 407 (1 strand) = 3 strands total

Use the same color thread to whip the chain stitches as shown below

Once the chain stitches are complete, pass a thread under each stitch without catching the fabric.

Vertical straight stitch

Horizontal straight stitch

Make groups of two long vertical straight stitches, then work short horizontal straight stitches on top as shown at right

435 (2 strands) + 407 (1 strand) = 3 strands total

Split 729

Satin 168

Back 3346

Split 3346

Split 3345

Seed Packet

SHOWN ON PAGE 9

MATERIALS

- DMC No. 25 embroidery floss in 320, 407, 729, 794, 844, 3328, 3346, 3347, 3689, 3806, 3838, 3865, and 3894
- DMC Pearl Cotton No. 5 in 3347
- Linen thread in green
- 6 × 12 in (15 × 30 cm) of white cotton sateen fabric
- 4 in (10 cm) square of blue linen fabric
- 2 × 4 in (5 × 10 cm) of green tulle
- 6 × 12 in (15 × 30 cm) of mid-weight fusible interfacing
- 4 in (10 cm) square of paper-backed fusible web
- Craft glue

MOTIF (shown at 100%)

- Use 2 strands unless otherwise noted.
- Use No. 25 embroidery floss unless otherwise noted.
- #25 = No. 25 embroidery floss and #5 = Pearl Cotton No. 5.

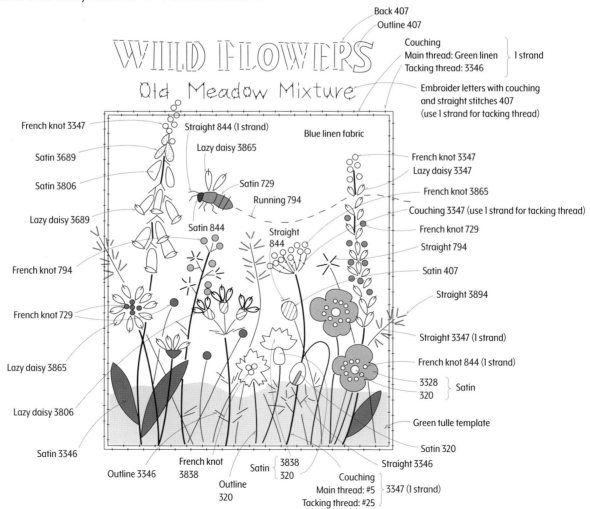

Back 407
Outline 407
Couching
Main thread: Green linen } 1 strand
Tacking thread: 3346
Embroider letters with couching and straight stitches 407 (use 1 strand for tacking thread)

French knot 3347
Satin 3689
Satin 3806
Lazy daisy 3689
French knot 794
French knot 729
Lazy daisy 3865
Lazy daisy 3806
Satin 3346

Straight 844 (1 strand)
Lazy daisy 3865
Satin 844
Satin 729
Running 794
Straight 844
Blue linen fabric

French knot 3347
Lazy daisy 3347
French knot 3865
Couching 3347 (use 1 strand for tacking thread)
French knot 729
Straight 794
Satin 407
Straight 3894
Straight 3347 (1 strand)
French knot 844 (1 strand)
3328
3320 } Satin
Green tulle template
Satin 320

Outline 3346
French knot 3838
Satin { 3838 / 320
Outline 320
Straight 3346
Couching
Main thread: #5
Tacking thread: #25 } 3347 (1 strand)

WILD FLOWERS
Old Meadow Mixture

INSTRUCTIONS

1. Adhere fusible interfacing to the wrong side of the white cotton sateen fabric.

2. Adhere paper-backed fusible web to the wrong side of the blue linen fabric. Trim the fabric down to 3 × 3½ in (7.5 × 9 cm). Remove the paper backing and adhere to the right side of the white cotton sateen fabric following the placement noted in the step 6 diagram at right.

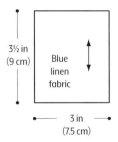

3. Transfer the embroidery motif onto the fabric.

4. Use the template on page 70 to cut the green tulle fabric into shape and position in place (it will be attached to the fabric by the embroidery).

5. Embroider the motif as noted in the diagram on page 70.

6. Once the embroidery is complete, use the template on Pattern Sheet B to trim the white cotton sateen fabric into shape. Apply glue to the left and right front edges.

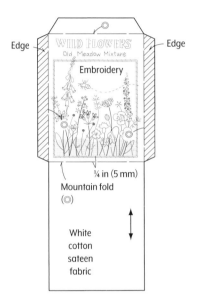

7. Fold the fabric into the packet shape.

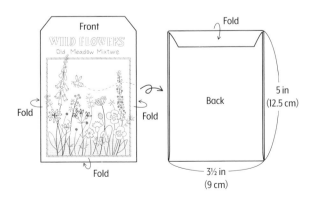

Violet Notebook

SHOWN ON PAGES 10–11

MATERIALS

- ⇝ DMC No. 25 embroidery floss in ECRU, 155, 168, 327, 368, 646, 729, 844, 939, 989, 3012, 3078, 3347, 3363, 3746, 3822, 3837, and 3862
- ⇝ DMC Pearl Cotton No. 5 in 989 and 3012
- ⇝ 11¾ × 25½ in (30 × 65 cm) of purple linen fabric
- ⇝ 12 × 33 in (30 × 84 cm) of white linen fabric
- ⇝ 17¾ × 25½ in (45 × 65 cm) of fusible fleece
- ⇝ 11 in (28 cm) of ⅛ in (3 mm) wide purple satin ribbon
- ⇝ Craft glue

INSTRUCTIONS

1. Cut a 11¼ × 14¾ in (28.5 × 37.5 cm) rectangle of purple linen fabric for the cover. Measure in 1½ in (3.5 cm) from each edge to mark the finishing lines on the wrong side of the fabric.

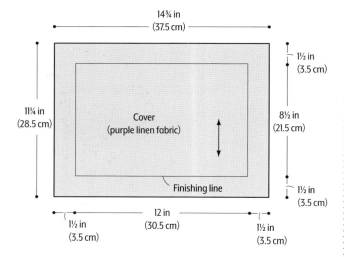

2. Cut a 8½ × 12 in (21.5 × 30.5 cm) rectangle of fusible fleece. Adhere to the wrong side of the cover along the marked finishing lines.

3. Miter the corners: Measure 1½ in (3.5 cm) from each corner and mark. Connect adjacent marks with a diagonal line. Cut along the diagonal lines to trim the corners. Fold each corner so the crease intersects with the finishing line corner point. Next, fold each side in along the marked finishing lines to complete the miter.

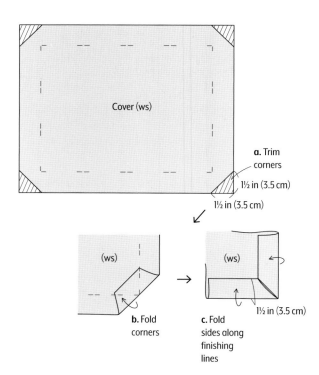

4. Cut a 7 × 10½ in (17.5 × 26.5 cm) rectangle of purple linen fabric for the cover lining.

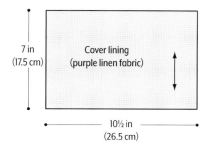

7 in
(17.5 cm)

Cover lining
(purple linen fabric)

10½ in
(26.5 cm)

5. Glue the ribbon to the wrong side of the cover at the center of the top edge. Glue the cover lining to the wrong side of the cover.

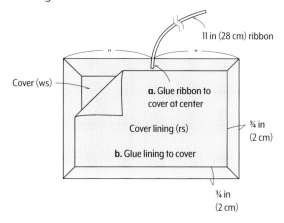

11 in (28 cm) ribbon

Cover (ws)

a. Glue ribbon to cover at center

Cover lining (rs)

b. Glue lining to cover

¾ in
(2 cm)

¾ in
(2 cm)

6. Adhere fusible fleece to the wrong side of the white linen fabric. Embroider the motif as noted in the diagrams on pages 74-75. Cut the white linen fabric into three 8¼ × 12 in (21 × 30 cm) rectangles as noted below. These will be the pages (one will be embroidered, while the other two will be blank).

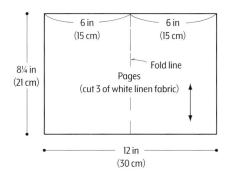

6 in
(15 cm)

6 in
(15 cm)

Fold line

8¼ in
(21 cm)

Pages
(cut 3 of white linen fabric)

12 in
(30 cm)

7. Align the two blank pages underneath the embroidered page. Fold in half at the center to crease. Running stitch along the crease to bind the three pages together.

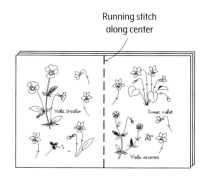

Running stitch
along center

Viola tricolor

Sweet violet

Viola arvensis

8. Apply glue to the crease on the wrong side of the bottom page. Adhere to the cover lining.

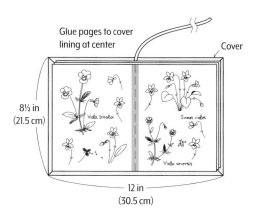

Glue pages to cover lining at center

Cover

8½ in
(21.5 cm)

Viola tricolor

Sweet violet

Viola arvensis

12 in
(30.5 cm)

MOTIF (shown at 100%)

- ⇝ Use 2 strands unless otherwise noted.
- ⇝ Use No. 25 embroidery floss unless otherwise noted.
- ⇝ #25 = No. 25 embroidery floss and #5 = Pearl Cotton No. 5.

Fold line

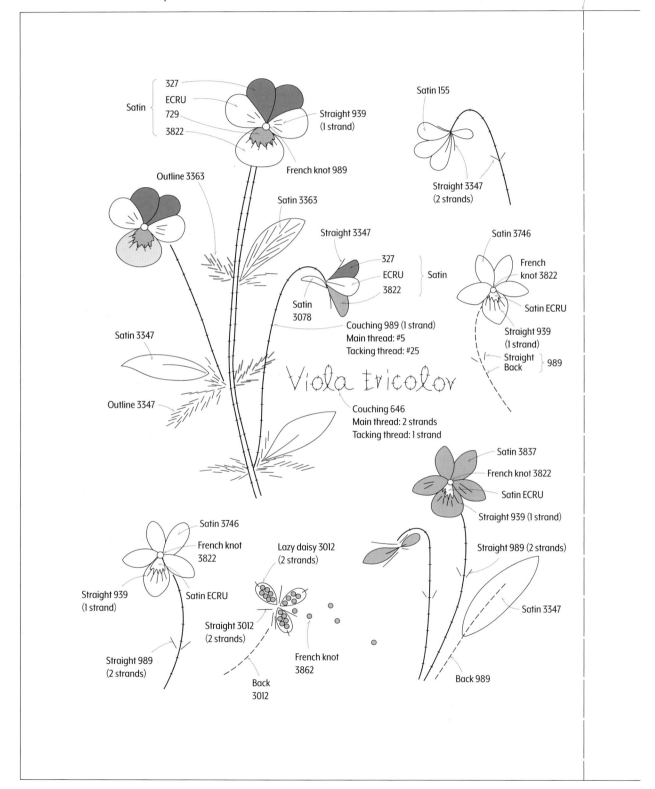

Satin
- 327
- ECRU
- 729
- 3822

Straight 939 (1 strand)

French knot 989

Satin 155

Straight 3347 (2 strands)

Outline 3363

Satin 3363

Satin 3746

Straight 3347

Satin
- 327
- ECRU
- 3822

French knot 3822

Satin ECRU

Satin 3078

Couching 989 (1 strand)
Main thread: #5
Tacking thread: #25

Straight 939 (1 strand)

Straight Back } 989

Satin 3347

Viola Tricolor

Outline 3347

Couching 646
Main thread: 2 strands
Tacking thread: 1 strand

Satin 3837

French knot 3822

Satin ECRU

Straight 939 (1 strand)

Straight 989 (2 strands)

Satin 3746

French knot 3822

Lazy daisy 3012 (2 strands)

Straight 939 (1 strand)

Satin ECRU

Satin 3347

Straight 3012 (2 strands)

French knot 3862

Straight 989 (2 strands)

Back 3012

Back 989

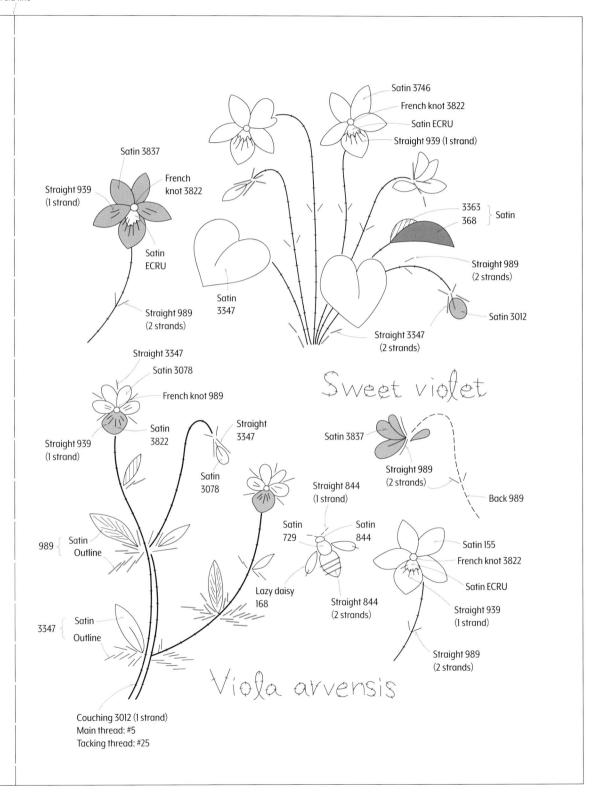

Satin 3837

Straight 939
(1 strand)

French
knot 3822

Satin
ECRU

Straight 989
(2 strands)

Satin 3746

French knot 3822

Satin ECRU

Straight 939 (1 strand)

3363
368 } Satin

Straight 989
(2 strands)

Satin 3012

Satin
3347

Straight 3347
(2 strands)

Sweet violet

Straight 3347

Satin 3078

French knot 989

Straight 939
(1 strand)

Satin
3822

Straight
3347

Satin
3078

Satin 3837

Straight 989
(2 strands)

Back 989

Straight 844
(1 strand)

Satin
729

Satin
844

Satin 155

French knot 3822

Satin ECRU

Straight 939
(1 strand)

989 } Satin
Outline

3347 } Satin
Outline

Lazy daisy
168

Straight 844
(2 strands)

Straight 989
(2 strands)

Viola arvensis

Couching 3012 (1 strand)
Main thread: #5
Tacking thread: #25

Rose Collage

SHOWN ON PAGE 12

MATERIALS

- DMC No. 25 embroidery floss in 151, 168, 368, 414, 434, 729, 760, 844, 931, 3064, 3346, 3347, 3354, 3805, 3816, 3821, 3865, 3894, and 4190
- DMC Pearl Cotton No. 5 in 3347
- 24 in (60 cm) of 1/8 in (3.5 mm) wide pink satin ribbon
- 13¾ × 15¾ in (35 × 40 cm) of beige linen fabric
- 13¾ × 21¾ in (35 × 55 mm) of mid-weight fusible interfacing
- 9¾ × 11¾ in (25 × 30 cm) of ¼ in (5 mm) thick foam board
- 1¼ × 2¾ in (3 × 7 cm) of green organdy fabric or ribbon
- 2¾ × 4¼ in (7 × 11 cm) of blue and white striped cotton fabric (for Motif C)
- 2¾ × 3¾ in (7 × 9.5 cm) of gray linen fabric (for Motif A)
- 2¾ in (7 cm) square of white linen fabric (for Motif B)
- 2 in (5 cm) square of pink polka dot cotton fabric (for Motif D)
- 1½ in (4 cm) square of white cotton fabric (for Motif A)
- 1½ in (4 cm) of paper-backed fusible web
- 2 × 3⅛ in (5 × 8 cm) of gray cotton fabric (for Motif E)
- ¾ × 1¼ in (2 × 3 cm) of white cardstock
- Invisible thread
- Craft glue
- Bookbinding tape

INSTRUCTIONS

1. Adhere fusible interfacing to the wrong side of the beige linen fabric.

2. Use the template on page 77 to cut the green organdy fabric or ribbon into shape. Appliqué to the beige linen fabric using invisible thread (refer to the diagram on page 77 for placement).

3. To make each motif, adhere fusible interfacing to the wrong side of each fabric. Embroider as noted in the diagrams on pages 77–78, and then trim into the finished shape.

4. Glue each motif to the beige linen fabric following the placement noted in the diagram on page 77.

5. To make the bobbin, wrap embroidery floss around the cardstock, and then glue to the beige linen fabric.

6. Once all of the motifs are complete, fold the beige linen fabric around the foam board. Use bookbinding tape to secure the fabric in place on the wrong side of the foam board.

FINISHED SIZE

9¾ × 11¾ in (25 × 30 cm)

MOTIF (shown on pages 77 and 78)

- Use 3 strands unless otherwise noted.
- Use No. 25 embroidery floss unless otherwise noted.
- #25 = No. 25 embroidery floss and #5 = Pearl Cotton No. 5.

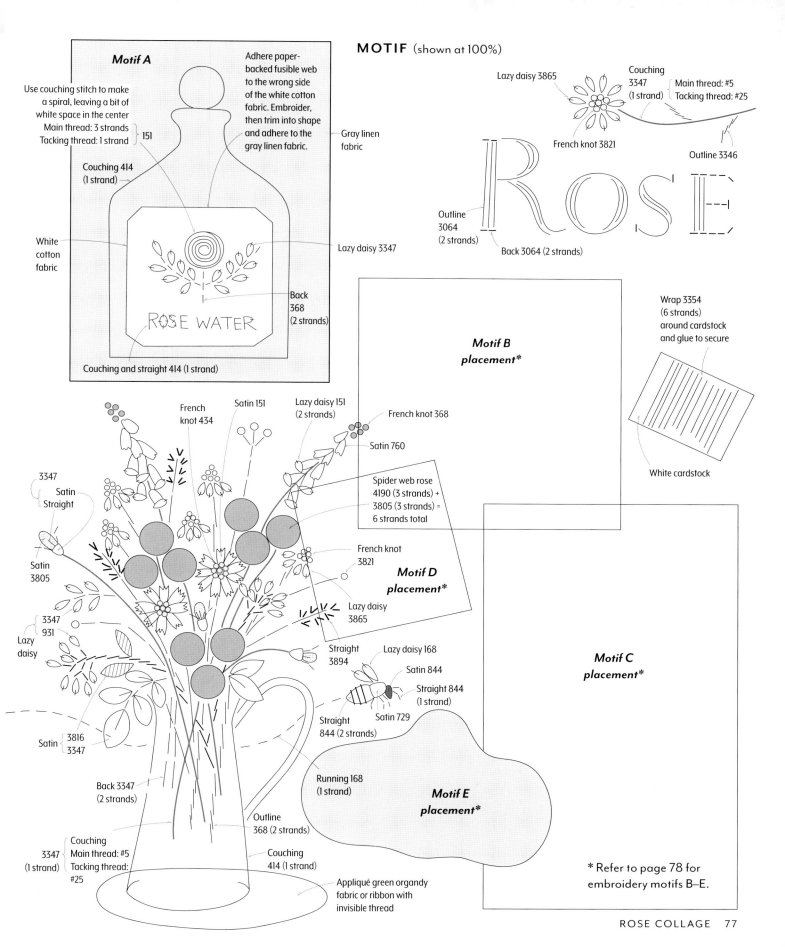

MOTIF (shown at 100%)

Motif A

Use couching stitch to make a spiral, leaving a bit of white space in the center
Main thread: 3 strands
Tacking thread: 1 strand

151

Adhere paper-backed fusible web to the wrong side of the white cotton fabric. Embroider, then trim into shape and adhere to the gray linen fabric.

Couching 414 (1 strand)

Gray linen fabric

White cotton fabric

Lazy daisy 3347

Back 368 (2 strands)

ROSE WATER

Couching and straight 414 (1 strand)

Lazy daisy 3865

Couching 3347 (1 strand)

Main thread: #5
Tacking thread: #25

French knot 3821

Outline 3346

Outline 3064 (2 strands)

Back 3064 (2 strands)

Motif B placement

Wrap 3354 (6 strands) around cardstock and glue to secure

White cardstock

3347 Satin Straight

Satin 3805

French knot 434

Satin 151

Lazy daisy 151 (2 strands)

French knot 368

Satin 760

Spider web rose 4190 (3 strands) + 3805 (3 strands) = 6 strands total

French knot 3821

Motif D placement

3347 931 Lazy daisy

Lazy daisy 3865

Straight 3894

Lazy daisy 168

Satin 844

Straight 844 (1 strand)

Straight 844 (2 strands)

Satin 729

Motif C placement

Satin 3816 3347

Back 3347 (2 strands)

Running 168 (1 strand)

Motif E placement

Outline 368 (2 strands)

3347 (1 strand) Couching
Main thread: #5
Tacking thread: #25

Couching 414 (1 strand)

Appliqué green organdy fabric or ribbon with invisible thread

* Refer to page 78 for embroidery motifs B–E.

MOTIF B

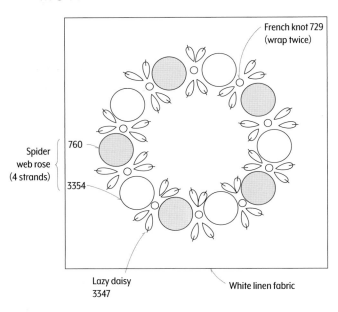

French knot 729
(wrap twice)

Spider
web rose
(4 strands)

760

3354

Lazy daisy
3347

White linen fabric

MOTIF C

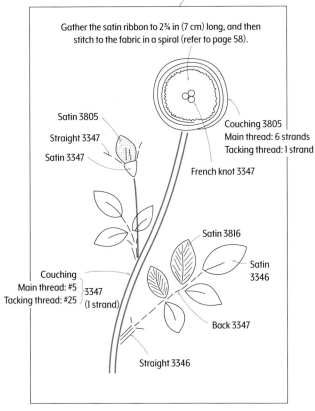

Blue and white striped
cotton fabric

Gather the satin ribbon to 2¾ in (7 cm) long, and then
stitch to the fabric in a spiral (refer to page 58).

Satin 3805

Straight 3347

Satin 3347

Couching 3805
Main thread: 6 strands
Tacking thread: 1 strand

French knot 3347

Satin 3816

Satin
3346

Back 3347

Couching
Main thread: #5
Tacking thread: #25
} 3347
(1 strand)

Straight 3346

MOTIF E

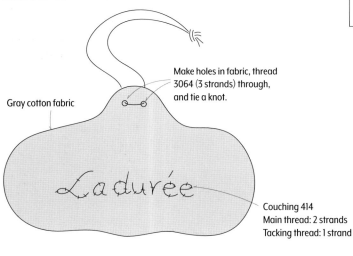

Gray cotton fabric

Make holes in fabric, thread
3064 (3 strands) through,
and tie a knot.

Ladurée

Couching 414
Main thread: 2 strands
Tacking thread: 1 strand

MOTIF D

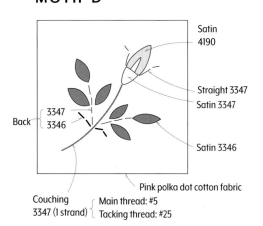

Satin
4190

Straight 3347

Satin 3347

Back { 3347
3346

Satin 3346

Pink polka dot cotton fabric

Couching
3347 (1 strand)

Main thread: #5
Tacking thread: #25

Rose Greeting Cards

SHOWN ON PAGE 13

MATERIALS

For Card A

- DMC No. 25 embroidery floss in 3363 and 4210
- 2¾ in (7 cm) square of text print cotton fabric
- 2¾ in (7 cm) square of mid-weight fusible interfacing
- 6 × 8¼ in (15 × 21 cm) of ivory Kent paper
- Craft glue

For Card B

- DMC No. 25 embroidery floss in 3346, 3347, and 4210
- DMC Pearl Cotton No. 5 in 3347
- 2 in (5 cm) square of pink polka dot cotton fabric
- 2 in (5 cm) square of mid-weight fusible interfacing
- 6 × 8¼ in (15 × 21 cm) of gray Kent paper
- Vintage postage stamps
- Scraps of print fabric or paper
- Craft glue

INSTRUCTIONS

1. Adhere fusible interfacing to the wrong side of the embroidery fabric.
2. Embroider as noted in the diagrams at right, and then trim into the finished shape.
3. Fold the Kent paper in half.
4. For card A, cut a 2⅜ in (6 cm) square window in the top layer of the Kent paper. Glue the embroidered fabric to the second layer of the Kent paper so it is visible through the window.
5. For card B, glue scraps of print fabric or paper, vintage postage stamps, and the embroidered fabric to the Kent paper as desired.

FINISHED SIZE

4⅛ × 6 in (10.5 × 15 cm)

MOTIFS (shown at 100%)

- Use 3 strands unless otherwise noted.
- Use No. 25 embroidery floss unless otherwise noted.
- #25 = No. 25 embroidery floss and #5 = Pearl Cotton No. 5.

Card A

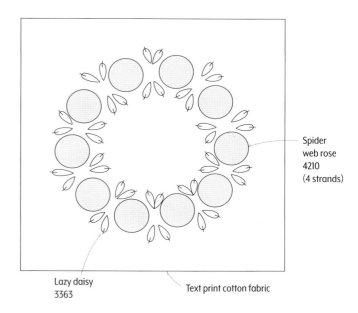

Spider web rose 4210 (4 strands)

Lazy daisy 3363

Text print cotton fabric

Card B

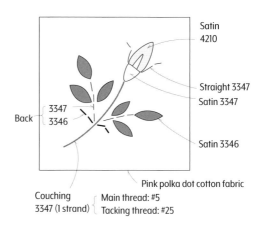

Satin 4210

Straight 3347

Satin 3347

Satin 3346

3347
3346

Back

Pink polka dot cotton fabric

Couching 3347 (1 strand) { Main thread: #5
Tacking thread: #25

Gardening Twine Cannister

SHOWN ON PAGE 19

MATERIALS

- → DMC No. 25 embroidery floss in ECRU, 729, and 844
- → 6 in (15 cm) square of beige linen fabric
- → 6 in (15 cm) square of mid-weight fusible interfacing
- → One 3⅛ in (8 cm) diameter embroidery hoop
- → ⅜ in (1 cm) diameter metal eyelet
- → Alphabet rubber stamps
- → Sepia ink pad (suitable for use on fabric)
- → Glass jar with a 3 in (7.5 cm) diameter

INSTRUCTIONS

1. Adhere fusible interfacing to the wrong side of the beige linen fabric.
2. Insert the fabric into the hoop and embroider as noted in the diagram below.
3. Remove from the hoop and install a metal eyelet at the center of the motif, as shown on page 64.
4. If desired, use the rubber stamps to add a circle of text around the eyelet.
5. Insert the work back into the hoop and trim any excess fabric.
6. Insert a roll of gardening twine into the glass jar. Thread the end of the twine through the eyelet, then snap the hoop into place on the glass jar.

FINISHED SIZE

3⅛ in (8 cm) diameter

MOTIF (shown at 100%)

- → Use 3 strands unless otherwise noted.

If your glass jar has a different diameter than the one called for in the materials list, make sure to adjust the size of your embroidery hoop accordingly—the hoop needs to be slightly larger than the jar opening in order to securely snap into place.

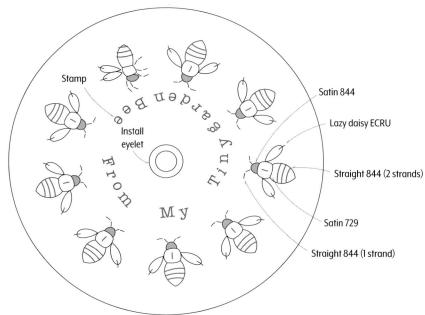

Bee Sampler

SHOWN ON PAGE 18

MATERIALS

- DMC No. 25 embroidery floss in ECRU, 156, 168, 320, 340, 341, 368, 677, 729, 822, and 844
- DMC Pearl Cotton No. 8 in ECRU and 644
- DMC Pearl Cotton No. 5 in 368
- 13 × 16¼ in (33 × 41 cm) of white linen fabric
- 13 × 16¼ in (33 × 41 cm) of mid-weight fusible interfacing
- 9 × 12¼ in (23 × 31 cm) of ¼ in (5 mm) thick foam board
- Bookbinding tape

INSTRUCTIONS

1. Adhere fusible interfacing to the wrong side of the white linen fabric.
2. Embroider as noted in the diagram on page 82.
3. Once the embroidery is complete, fold the white linen fabric around the foam board. Use bookbinding tape to secure the fabric in place on the wrong side of the foam board.

FINISHED SIZE

9 × 12¼ in (23 × 31 cm)

Display this sampler in a shadow box frame or tray to capture the look of a scientific insect collection, as shown on page 18. Simply adjust the size of the foam board to match the frame or tray.

MOTIF (shown on page 82)

- Use 3 strands unless otherwise noted.
- Use No. 25 embroidery floss unless otherwise noted.
- #25 = No. 25 embroidery floss, while #5 = Pearl Cotton No. 5 and #8 = Pearl Cotton No. 8.

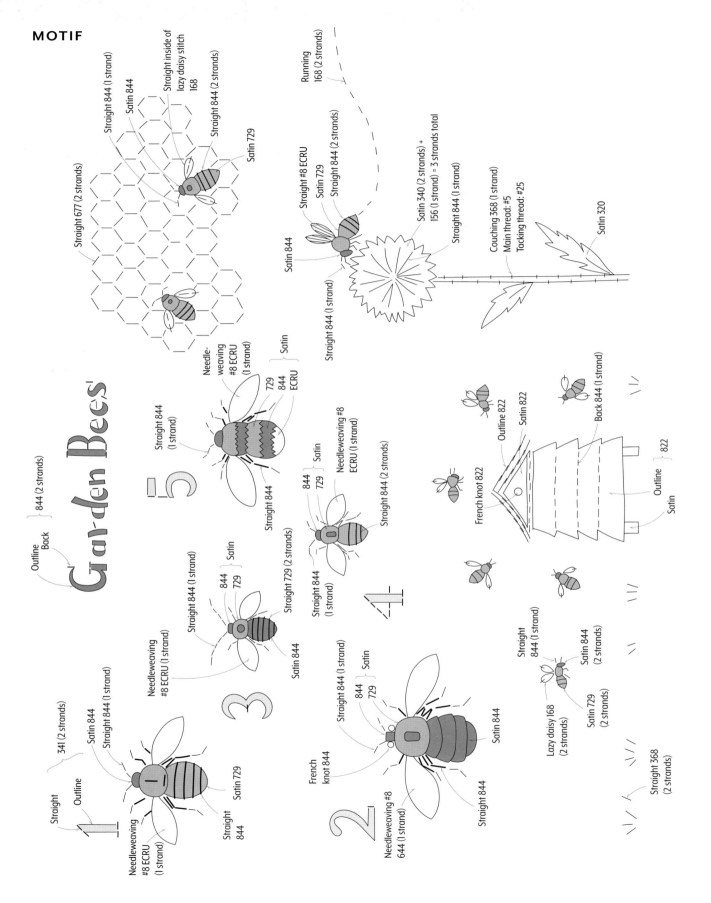

Garden Bees

Outline { Back { 844 (2 strands)

1
Straight { Outline
Needleweaving #8 ECRU (1 strand)
Straight 341 (2 strands)
Satin 844
Straight 844 (1 strand)
Straight 844
Satin 729

3
Needleweaving #8 ECRU (1 strand)
Straight 844 (1 strand)
Satin 844
844 } Satin
729
Straight 729 (2 strands)

Needleweaving #8 ECRU (1 strand)
Needleweaving #8 ECRU (1 strand)
Straight 844 (1 strand)
729 } Satin
844 } ECRU
Straight 844

844 } Satin
729
Needleweaving #8 ECRU (1 strand)
Straight 844 (1 strand)
Straight 844 (2 strands)

2
Needleweaving #8 644 (1 strand)
Straight 844 (1 strand)
844 } Satin
729
French knot 844
Satin 844
Straight 844

Lazy daisy 168 (2 strands)
Satin 729 (2 strands)
Straight 844 (1 strand)
Satin 844 (2 strands)

French knot 822
Outline 822
Satin 822
Outline } 822
Satin
Back 844 (1 strand)

Straight 368 (2 strands)

Straight 677 (2 strands)
Straight 844 (1 strand)
Satin 844
Straight inside of lazy daisy stitch 168
Straight 844 (2 strands)
Satin 729

Running 168 (2 strands)
Straight #8 ECRU
Satin 729
Straight 844 (2 strands)
Satin 844
Straight 844 (1 strand)
Satin 340 (2 strands) + 156 (1 strand) = 3 strands total
Straight 844 (1 strand)
Couching 368 (1 strand) Main thread: #5 Tacking thread: #25
Satin 320

Garden Sampler

SHOWN ON PAGES 14–15

MATERIALS

- DMC No. 25 embroidery floss in ECRU, 156, 168, 368, 554, 729, 760, 761, 844, 907, 937, 988, 989, 3328, 3607, 3805, 3822, 3862, and 3894
- DMC Pearl Cotton No. 5 in 368, 988, and 989
- Linen thread in green, yellow green, and purple (Note: If you don't have linen thread, try using three stands of DMC No. 25 embroidery floss in 988, 3894, and 554 respectively.)
- 15¾ × 19 in (40 × 48 cm) of white linen fabric
- 15¾ × 19 in (40 × 48 cm) of mid-weight fusible interfacing
- 11¾ × 15 in (30 × 38 cm) of ¼ in (5 mm) thick foam board
- 4 × 11¾ in (10 × 30 cm) of dark green tulle
- 15¾ in (40 cm) of wire
- Invisible thread
- Bookbinding tape

INSTRUCTIONS

1. Adhere fusible interfacing to the wrong side of the white linen fabric.

2. Use the templates on pages 84–85 to cut the dark green tulle into shape. Appliqué to the white linen fabric using invisible thread.

3. Bend the wire into shape following the template on page 84. Appliqué to the white linen fabric using invisible thread.

4. Transfer the embroidery motif on pages 84–85 to your fabric. Embroider as noted in the Stitch Guide on pages 86–87.

5. Once the embroidery is complete, fold the white linen fabric around the foam board. Use bookbinding tape to secure the fabric in place on the wrong side of the foam board.

FINISHED SIZE

11¾ × 15 in (30 × 38 cm)

MOTIF (shown at 100%)

⇾ Refer to pages 86–87 for stitching instructions.

Align notches

STITCH GUIDE (NOT A TEMPLATE)

- Use 2 strands unless otherwise noted.
- Use No. 25 embroidery floss unless otherwise noted.
- #25 = No. 25 embroidery floss and #5 = Pearl Cotton No. 5.

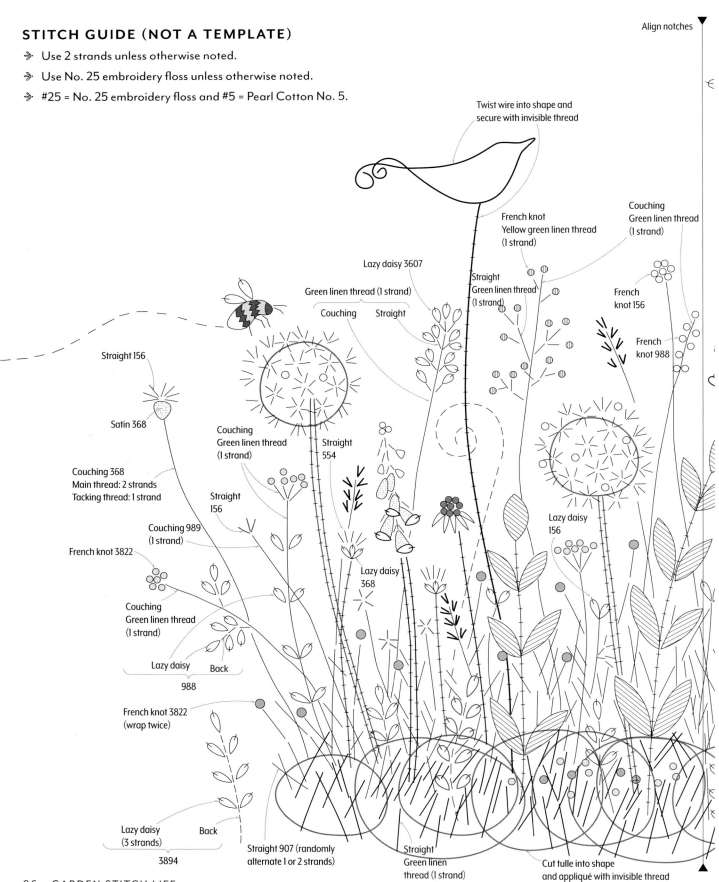

Align notches

Twist wire into shape and secure with invisible thread

French knot
Yellow green linen thread (1 strand)

Couching
Green linen thread (1 strand)

Lazy daisy 3607

Green linen thread (1 strand)

Straight
Green linen thread (1 strand)

French knot 156

Couching   Straight

French knot 988

Straight 156

Satin 368

Couching
Green linen thread (1 strand)

Straight
554

Couching 368
Main thread: 2 strands
Tacking thread: 1 strand

Straight
156

Couching 989
(1 strand)

French knot 3822

Lazy daisy 156

Couching
Green linen thread (1 strand)

Lazy daisy
368

Lazy daisy   Back

988

French knot 3822
(wrap twice)

Lazy daisy
(3 strands)   Back

3894

Straight 907 (randomly alternate 1 or 2 strands)

Straight
Green linen thread (1 strand)

Cut tulle into shape and appliqué with invisible thread

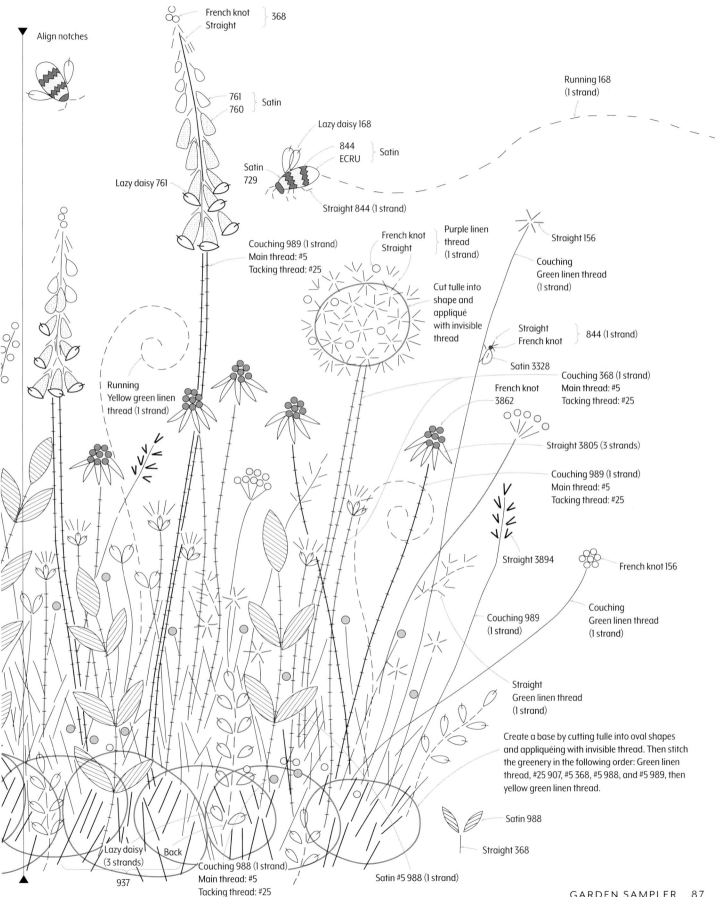

Align notches

French knot
Straight } 368

761
760 } Satin

Running 168
(1 strand)

Lazy daisy 168

844
ECRU } Satin

Satin
729

Lazy daisy 761

Straight 844 (1 strand)

Couching 989 (1 strand)
Main thread: #5
Tacking thread: #25

French knot
Straight

Purple linen
thread
(1 strand)

Straight 156

Couching
Green linen thread
(1 strand)

Cut tulle into
shape and
appliqué
with invisible
thread

Straight
French knot } 844 (1 strand)

Satin 3328

Running
Yellow green linen
thread (1 strand)

French knot
3862

Couching 368 (1 strand)
Main thread: #5
Tacking thread: #25

Straight 3805 (3 strands)

Couching 989 (1 strand)
Main thread: #5
Tacking thread: #25

Straight 3894

French knot 156

Couching 989
(1 strand)

Couching
Green linen thread
(1 strand)

Straight
Green linen thread
(1 strand)

Create a base by cutting tulle into oval shapes
and appliquéing with invisible thread. Then stitch
the greenery in the following order: Green linen
thread, #25 907, #5 368, #5 988, and #5 989, then
yellow green linen thread.

Satin 988

Straight 368

Lazy daisy
(3 strands)

937

Back

Couching 988 (1 strand)
Main thread: #5
Tacking thread: #25

Satin #5 988 (1 strand)

Alphabet Sampler

SHOWN ON PAGES 16–17

MATERIALS

- DMC No. 25 embroidery floss in 435, 612, 645, 794, 989, and 4050
- Linen thread in beige
- 17 × 21¾ in (43 × 55 cm) of white linen fabric
- 17 × 21¾ in (43 × 55 cm) of mid-weight fusible interfacing
- 4¾ × 8 in (12 × 20 cm) of cheesecloth
- ¾ × 1½ in (2 × 3.5 cm) of text print fabric
- Acrylic paint in white and beige
- 13 × 17¾ in (33 × 45 cm) of ¼ in (5 mm) thick foam board
- Bookbinding tape

INSTRUCTIONS

1. Adhere fusible interfacing to the wrong side of the white linen fabric.

2. Use the templates on Pattern Sheet A to cut the pieces of cheesecloth and text print fabric into shape. Appliqué to the white linen fabric using a free motion quilting setting on the sewing machine.

3. Mix a small amount of beige with the white acrylic paint, and then apply to the appliquéd fabric.

4. Once the paint dries, embroider as noted in the diagram on Pattern Sheet A.

5. Once the embroidery is complete, fold the white linen fabric around the foam board. Use bookbinding tape to secure the fabric in place on the wrong side of the foam board.

FINISHED SIZE

13 × 17¾ in (33 × 45 cm)

Spring Flowers Doily

SHOWN ON PAGE 20

MATERIALS

➤ DMC No. 25 embroidery floss in ECRU, 155, 157, 320, 368, 472, 554, 939, 989, 3078, 3781, 3821, and 3839

➤ 10¾ in (27 cm) square of white linen fabric

INSTRUCTIONS

1. Embroider the motif as noted in the diagram on Pattern Sheet A.

2. Mark the finishing lines. Backstitch ⅜ in (1 cm) inside the finishing lines using three strands of ECRU floss.

3. Trim the fabric into a 10¾ in (27 cm) square.

4. Miter the corners and finish the edges as shown on page 64.

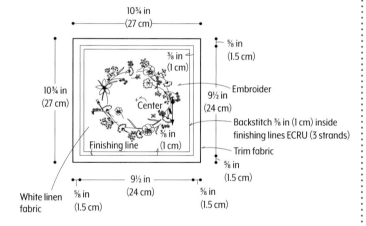

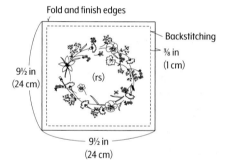

A Letter to Spring

SHOWN ON PAGE 21

MATERIALS

- ➢ DMC No. 25 embroidery floss in ECRU, 168, 327, 644, 729, 844, 939, 989, 3348, 3820, and 3822
- ➢ DMC Pearl Cotton No. 5 in 989
- ➢ 10¼ × 12¼ in (26 × 31 cm) of white linen fabric
- ➢ 10¼ × 12¼ in (26 × 31 cm) of mid-weight fusible interfacing
- ➢ 1 × 3 in (2.5 × 7.5 cm) of text print fabric
- ➢ 2 × 2⅜ in (5 × 6 cm) of cheesecloth
- ➢ ⅝ × 1½ in (1.5 × 4 cm) label
- ➢ Craft glue
- ➢ Acrylic paint in white and beige

INSTRUCTIONS

1. Adhere fusible interfacing to the wrong side of the white linen fabric.

2. Use the templates on page 91 to cut the pieces of cheesecloth and text print fabric into shape. Appliqué to the white linen fabric using a free motion quilting setting on the sewing machine.

3. Mix a small amount of beige with the white acrylic paint, and then apply to the appliquéd fabric.

4. Once the paint dries, embroider as noted in the diagram on page 91.

5. Once the embroidery is complete, use the template on Pattern Sheet A to cut the white linen fabric into the shape shown below.

6. Fold the fabric into the envelope shape following the numerical order listed below, then glue to secure. Glue the label to the front (refer to the template on page 91 for placement).

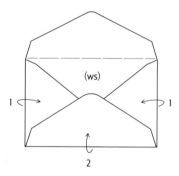

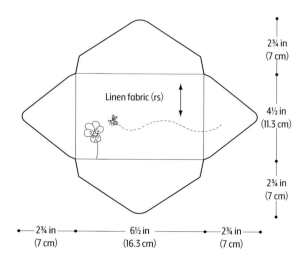

MOTIF (shown at 100%)

- ❧ Use 3 strands unless otherwise noted.
- ❧ Use No. 25 embroidery floss unless otherwise noted.
- ❧ #25 = No. 25 embroidery floss and #5 = Pearl Cotton No. 5.

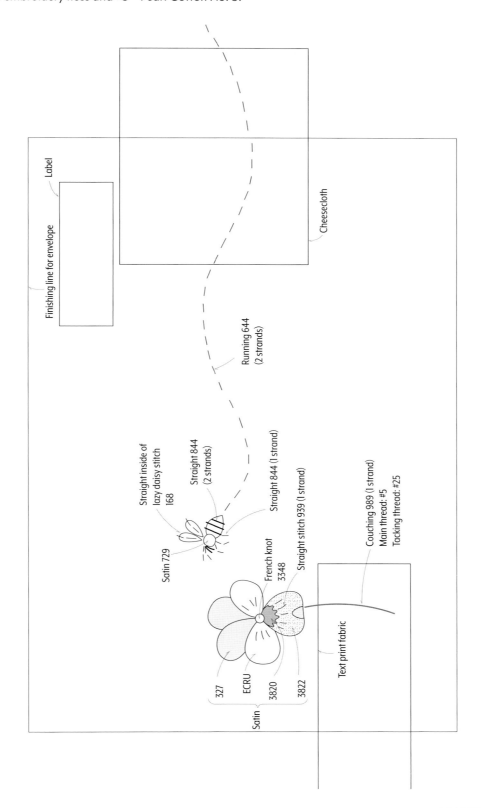

Label

Finishing line for envelope

Cheesecloth

Running 644
(2 strands)

Straight inside of
lazy daisy stitch
168

Straight 844
(2 strands)

Straight 844 (1 strand)

Satin 729

French knot
3348

Straight stitch 939 (1 strand)

Couching 989 (1 strand)
Main thread: #5
Tacking thread: #25

327

ECRU

3820

3822

Satin

Text print fabric

Garden Visitors

SHOWN ON PAGE 22

MATERIALS

- ⇝ DMC No. 25 embroidery floss in 341, 676, 822, 977, 3790, and 3799
- ⇝ Linen thread in dark brown
- ⇝ 9¾ × 11¾ in (25 × 30 cm) of gray linen fabric
- ⇝ 4 × 11¾ in (10 × 30 cm) of beige linen/cotton blend fabric
- ⇝ 11¾ × 13¾ in (30 × 35 cm) of mid-weight fusible interfacing
- ⇝ 8 × 9¾ in (20 × 25 cm) of ¼ in (5 mm) thick foam board
- ⇝ Bookbinding tape

INSTRUCTIONS

1. Align the beige linen fabric beneath the gray linen fabric, then adhere fusible interfacing to the wrong side of the combined fabric. On the right side, zigzag stitch on top of the joint line (refer to the template on page 93 for placement).

2. Embroider as noted in the diagram on page 93.

3. Once the embroidery is complete, fold the fabric around the foam board. Use bookbinding tape to secure the fabric in place on the wrong side of the foam board.

FINISHED SIZE

8 × 9¾ in (20 × 25 cm)

MOTIF (shown at 100%)

⇾ Use 3 strands unless otherwise noted.

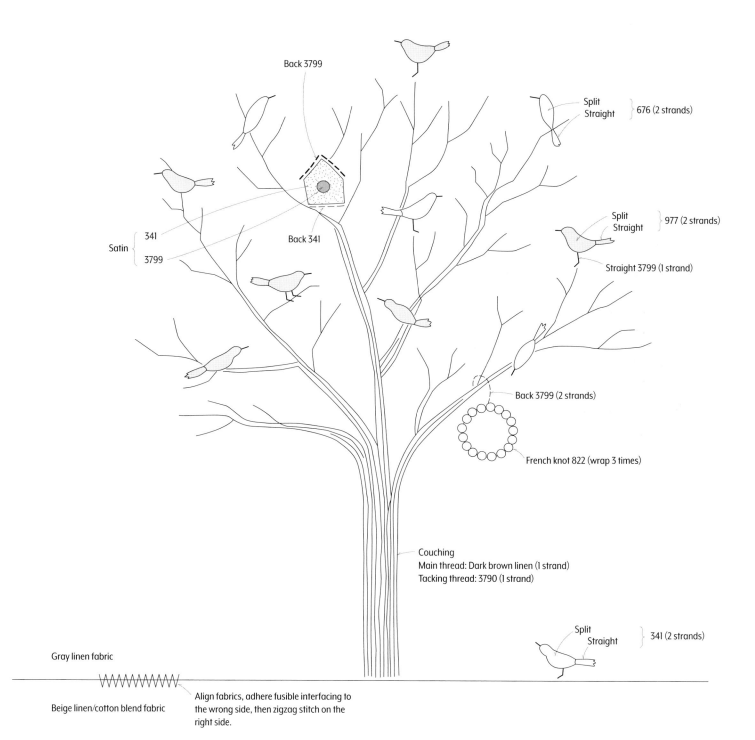

Back 3799

Split Straight } 676 (2 strands)

Split Straight } 977 (2 strands)

Straight 3799 (1 strand)

341
Satin {
3799

Back 341

Back 3799 (2 strands)

French knot 822 (wrap 3 times)

Couching
Main thread: Dark brown linen (1 strand)
Tacking thread: 3790 (1 strand)

Split Straight } 341 (2 strands)

Gray linen fabric

Beige linen/cotton blend fabric

Align fabrics, adhere fusible interfacing to the wrong side, then zigzag stitch on the right side.

Bird Studies

SHOWN ON PAGE 23

MATERIALS (FOR ONE BIRD)

- DMC No. 25 embroidery floss in ECRU, 169, 310, 610, 921, and 3865 for robin and ECRU, 310, 420, and 839 for fieldfare
- 6 in (15 cm) square of white linen fabric
- 6 in (15 cm) square of mid-weight fusible interfacing
- 3⅛ × 4¾ in (8 × 12 cm) of beige felt
- Craft glue
- Wire
- Brooch pin (optional)

INSTRUCTIONS

1. Adhere fusible interfacing to the wrong side of the white linen fabric.

2. Embroider as noted in the diagram below.

3. Cut out the embroidered design, leaving a ⅜ in (8 mm) margin.

4. Cut small notches into the margin along the curved areas, then fold the margin back and glue it to the wrong side of the embroidery, as shown on page 62.

5. Cut a piece of felt in the size and shape of the finished embroidery. Bend a short piece of wire for the beak and glue the wire to the wrong side of the embroidery. If using as a decoration, cut and glue a long piece of wire to the wrong side, then sew the felt to the embroidery as shown on page 62. Or if you'd prefer to wear the design as a brooch, skip the wire and glue a brooch pin to the felt backing instead.

MOTIFS (shown at 100%)

- Use 3 strands unless otherwise noted.

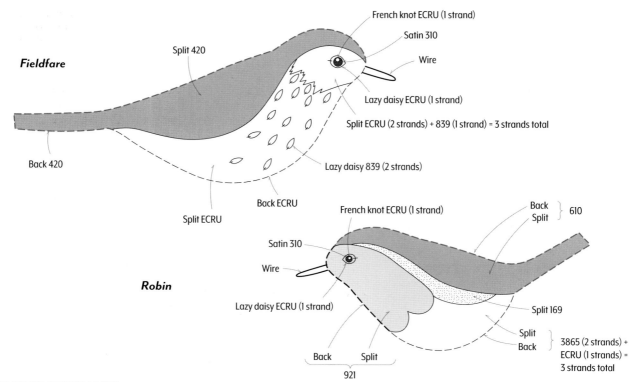

Acorn Knitting Needles

SHOWN ON PAGE 25

MATERIALS

- DMC No. 25 embroidery floss in 898
- DMC Pearl Cotton No. 5 in 3045
- Brown wool roving
- Felting needle
- Craft glue

- Double-pointed knitting needles in desired size (for the knitting needles only)
- 2¾ in (7 cm) of ⅛ in (2.5 mm) wide brown ribbon or leather cord (for the ornament only)

INSTRUCTIONS

1. Use a felting needle to form the brown wool roving into a 1 in (2.5 cm) acorn shape. Refer to the guide on page 63 for step-by-step photos showing how to make the acorn.

2. Use a knitting needle to poke a hole through the center of the acorn. Remove the knitting needle.

3. Work five rows of the buttonhole stitch.

4. Make a bullion knot.

5. Apply craft glue to one end of the knitting needle. Insert into the hole from step 2. Let the glue dry.

6. Repeat steps 1–5 to make the other knitting needle.

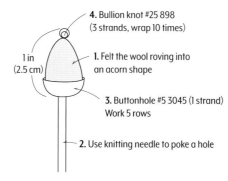

4. Bullion knot #25 898
(3 strands, wrap 10 times)

1 in
(2.5 cm)

1. Felt the wool roving into an acorn shape

3. Buttonhole #5 3045 (1 strand)
Work 5 rows

2. Use knitting needle to poke a hole

Variation

The acorn design can also be used to make an ornament or pin cushion. To make an ornament, complete steps 1–4 as listed at left, then follow the instructions below to attach a ribbon or leather loop.

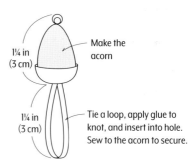

1¼ in
(3 cm)

Make the acorn

1¼ in
(3 cm)

Tie a loop, apply glue to knot, and insert into hole. Sew to the acorn to secure.

To make a pin cushion, complete steps 1, 3, and 4 as listed at left, then follow the instructions below. You could also insert a piece of a dowel or twig, as shown on page 45.

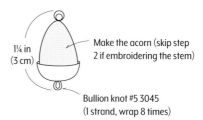

1¼ in
(3 cm)

Make the acorn (skip step 2 if embroidering the stem)

Bullion knot #5 3045
(1 strand, wrap 8 times)

Wool prevents rust from forming on metal, so this design makes for an excellent pin cushion or needle minder.

Fall Field Samples

SHOWN ON PAGE 24

MATERIALS

→ DMC No. 25 embroidery floss in ECRU, 347, 349, 420, 433, 434, 833, 841, 3782, and 4130

→ 12 in (30 cm) square of white linen fabric

→ 12 in (30 cm) square of mid-weight fusible interfacing

→ ¼ in (6 mm) wide beige organdy ribbon

→ Number and letter rubber stamps

→ Sepia ink pad (suitable for use on fabric)

→ Craft glue

INSTRUCTIONS

1. Adhere fusible interfacing to the wrong side of the white linen fabric.

2. Embroider the motifs as noted in the diagrams below and on page 97.

3. If desired, stamp the number labels in the top left corner of each motif.

4. Cut each motif out along the marked rectangles.

> To make any of these designs into a brooch, refer to the guide on page 62. You will need felt, craft glue, and a brooch pin.

MOTIFS (shown at 100%)

→ Use 3 strands unless otherwise noted.

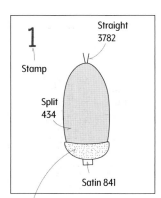

1 — Stamp — Straight 3782 — Split 434 — Satin 841

Detached buttonhole
3782 (4 strands)

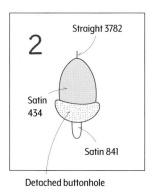

2 — Straight 3782 — Satin 434 — Satin 841

Detached buttonhole
3782 (4 strands)

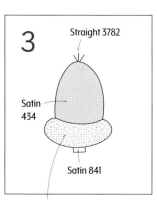

3 — Straight 3782 — Satin 434 — Satin 841

Detached buttonhole
3782 (4 strands)

4 — Straight 841 — Split 434 — Satin 841

Detached buttonhole
3782 (4 strands)

> ### How to Work the Detached Buttonhole Stitch
>
>
>
> 3rd row → ← Lazy daisy stitch
> 1st row → ← 2nd row
>
> Start each row with a lazy daisy stitch, then continue by making buttonhole stitches. For the second row, work the previous row of stitches without catching the fabric. Go back to inserting the needle through the fabric when making the buttonhole stitches for the third row.

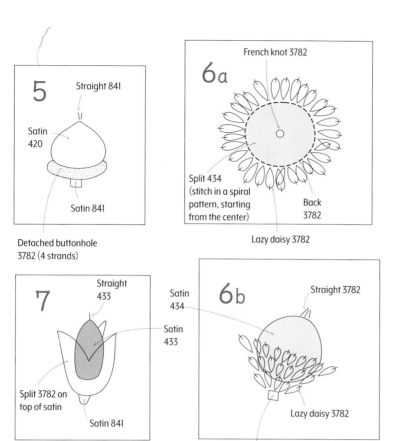

5

Straight 841

Satin 420

Satin 841

Detached buttonhole 3782 (4 strands)

6a

French knot 3782

Split 434 (stitch in a spiral pattern, starting from the center)

Back 3782

Lazy daisy 3782

7

Straight 433

Satin 433

Split 3782 on top of satin

Satin 841

6b

Satin 434

Straight 3782

Lazy daisy 3782

Satin 841

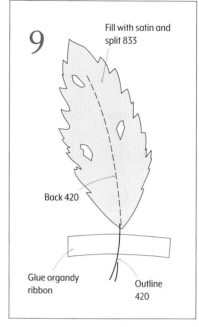

9

Fill with satin and split 833

Back 420

Glue organdy ribbon

Outline 420

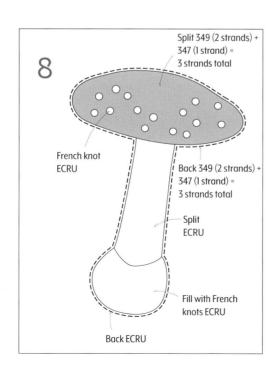

8

Split 349 (2 strands) + 347 (1 strand) = 3 strands total

French knot ECRU

Back 349 (2 strands) + 347 (1 strand) = 3 strands total

Split ECRU

Fill with French knots ECRU

Back ECRU

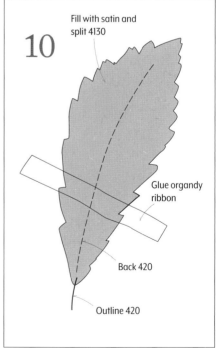

10

Fill with satin and split 4130

Glue organdy ribbon

Back 420

Outline 420

Chamomile Sachet

SHOWN ON PAGE 26

MATERIALS

- DMC No. 25 embroidery floss in 3346, 3347, 3747, 3821, and 3865
- 6¼ × 15¾ in (16 × 40 cm) of beige linen fabric
- 19¾ in (50 cm) of ¼ in (6 mm) wide beige linen tape
- Brass bee charm
- Alphabet rubber stamps
- Brown ink pad (suitable for use on fabric)

INSTRUCTIONS

1. Cut a 6¼ × 15¾ in (16 × 40 cm) rectangle of beige linen fabric.

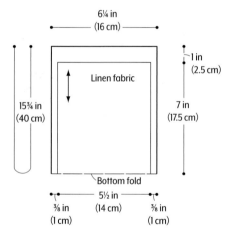

2. Embroider, stamp, and attach the charm as noted in the diagram on page 99. If it's too difficult to transfer the embroidery motif onto the fabric due to the rough texture of the linen, try using a sheet of freezer paper, as shown on page 60.

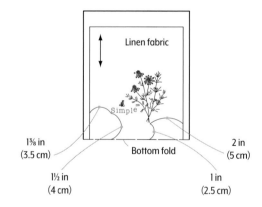

3. Zigzag stitch around all four sides of the fabric to finish the raw edges. Fold in half with right sides together. Use ⅜ in (1 cm) seam allowance to sew along the sides, stitching 5½ in (14 cm) long seams, as measured from the bottom fold.

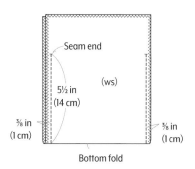

Seam end

5½ in
(14 cm)

(ws)

⅜ in
(1 cm)

⅜ in
(1 cm)

Bottom fold

4. Press the seam allowances open. Fold and press the seam allowances to the wrong side above the seam ends from step 3. Topstitch in a V-shape as noted below. Next, fold and press the top edge down 1 in (2.5 cm). From the right side of the bag, topstitch ⅝ in (1.5 cm) from the top fold to create the casing. Thread the linen tape through the casing and knot the ends together.

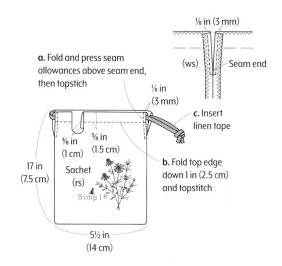

⅛ in (3 mm)

(ws)   Seam end

a. Fold and press seam allowances above seam end, then topstich

⅛ in
(3 mm)

c. Insert linen tape

17 in
(7.5 cm)

⅜ in
(1 cm)

⅝ in
(1.5 cm)

Sachet
(rs)

Simple

b. Fold top edge down 1 in (2.5 cm) and topstitch

5½ in
(14 cm)

MOTIF (shown at 100%)

✥ Use 3 strands unless otherwise noted.

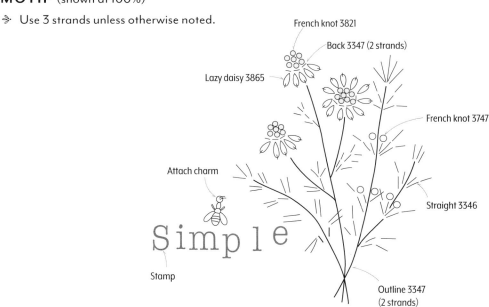

French knot 3821

Back 3347 (2 strands)

Lazy daisy 3865

French knot 3747

Attach charm

Straight 3346

Simple

Stamp

Outline 3347
(2 strands)

Foldover Clutch

SHOWN ON PAGE 26

MATERIALS

- → DMC No. 25 embroidery floss in 3346 and 3347
- → 16¼ × 27½ in (41 × 70 cm) of beige linen fabric
- → 6 × 13¾ in (15 × 35 cm) of striped cotton fabric
- → 27½ in (70 cm) of beige picot lace
- → Alphabet rubber stamps
- → Brown ink pad (suitable for use on fabric)

INSTRUCTIONS

1. Cut two 13¾ × 16¼ in (35 × 41 cm) rectangles of beige linen fabric for the bag outsides and two 3 × 13¾ in (7.5 × 35 cm) rectangles of striped cotton fabric for the facings.

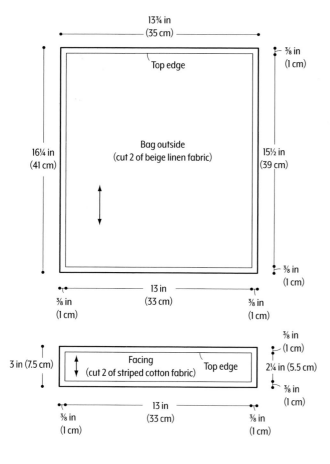

2. Embroider the motif onto one of the bag outsides, as noted in the diagram on page 101. If desired, stamp the embroidered fabric. With right sides together, align each facing with the top edge of a bag outside. Sandwich a piece of lace in between the layers of fabric and sew together using ⅜ in (1 cm) seam allowance.

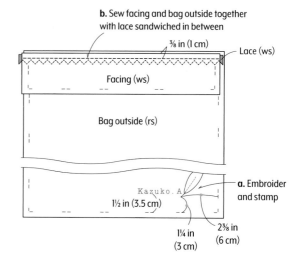

3. Fold the facing to the wrong side of the bag outside, so the lace points upward. Topstitch as close to the lace as possible. Fold and press the bottom seam allowance of the facing under. From the right side of the bag, topstitch the facing in place as noted below. Zigzag stitch around the sides and bottom to finish the raw edges. Repeat for the other half of the bag.

$\frac{1}{16}$ in (2 mm)

a. Fold facing to inside and topstitch

2 in (5 cm)

b. Fold seam allowance under and topstitch

Bag outside (rs)

c. Zigzag stitch sides and bottom

Kazuko.A

4. Align the two bag outsides with right sides together. Sew around the sides and bottom using ⅜ in (1 cm) seam allowance. Turn the bag right side out.

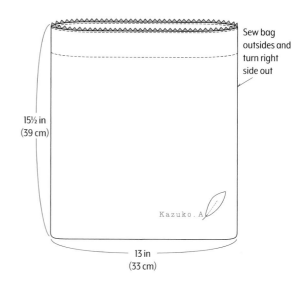

Sew bag outsides and turn right side out

15½ in (39 cm)

Kazuko.A

13 in (33 cm)

MOTIF (shown at 100%)

➤ Use 3 strands unless otherwise noted.

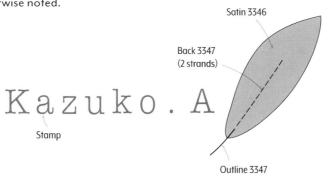

Kazuko.A

Stamp

Satin 3346

Back 3347 (2 strands)

Outline 3347

Pottery Placemat

SHOWN ON PAGE 34

MATERIALS

↷ DMC No. 25 embroidery floss in 3799

↷ 9¾ × 13¾ in (25 × 35 cm) of beige linen fabric

FINISHED SIZE

8 × 11¾ in (20 × 30 cm)

MOTIF (shown at 100%)

↷ Use 3799 (2 strands) for entire motif.

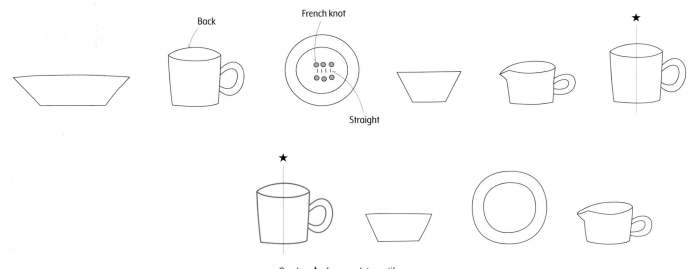

INSTRUCTIONS

1. Cut a 9¾ × 13¾ in (25 × 35 cm) rectangle of beige linen fabric. Mark the finishing lines 1 in (2.5 cm) from each edge. Embroider the motif as noted in the diagram on page 102. Backstitch along the finishing lines.

13¾ in
(35 cm)

Linen fabric

3½ in
(9 cm) **Embroidery placement**

a. Embroider

b. Back 3799
(3 strands)

1 in
(2.5 cm)

8 in
(20 cm)

9¾ in
(25 cm)

¾ in
(2 cm)

Finishing line

1 in
(2.5 cm)

11¾ in
(30 cm)

1 in
(2.5 cm)

1 in
(2.5 cm)

2. Fold and press the seam allowances in ⅜ in (1 cm), then ⅝ in (1.5 cm) to miter the corners, as shown in the guide below. Note: Once the seam allowances are folded into place, the backstitching from step 1 will become an edging around the placemat. Use the sewing machine to topstitch the hem in place, stitching ½ in (1.2 cm) from the edge. Hand stitch the mitered corner folds together.

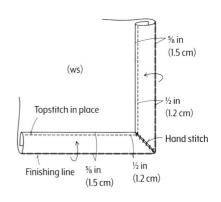

⅝ in
(1.5 cm)

(ws)

½ in
(1.2 cm)

Topstitch in place

Hand stitch

Finishing line

⅝ in
(1.5 cm)

½ in
(1.2 cm)

How to Miter the Corners

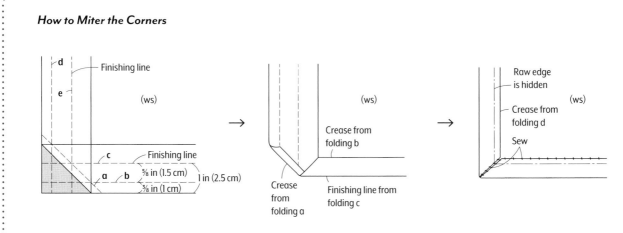

d

e

Finishing line

(ws)

c

Finishing line

a b

⅝ in (1.5 cm)

1 in (2.5 cm)

⅜ in (1 cm)

(ws)

Crease from folding b

Crease from folding a

Finishing line from folding c

Raw edge is hidden

(ws)

Crease from folding d

Sew

1. Trim corners, leaving ⅜ in (1 cm) seam allowance from the finishing line.

2. Start by folding a–c.

3. Next, fold d and e. Hand stitch or topstitch the hem in place, stitching the mitered corner folds in place as you work.

Market Bag

SHOWN ON PAGE 35

MATERIALS

→ DMC No. 25 embroidery floss in 3799

→ 19¾ × 31½ in (50 × 80 cm) of beige linen fabric

→ 2 yds (1.8 m) of ¼ in (6 mm) wide black double fold bias tape

MOTIF (shown at 100%)

→ Use 3799 (2 strands) for entire motif.

→ Backstitch unless otherwise noted.

Center

Split

French knot

Lazy daisy

FINLAND

INSTRUCTIONS

1. Cut two bag sides using the template on Pattern Sheet B (do not add seam allowance). Zigzag stitch as shown to finish the raw edges. Embroider one of the bag sides as noted in the diagram on page 104.

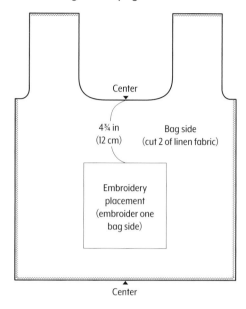

Center

4¾ in (12 cm)

Bag side (cut 2 of linen fabric)

Embroidery placement (embroider one bag side)

Center

2. Bind the curved edges as shown in the diagram below. Then align the two bag sides with right sides together. Sew together along the sides using ⅜ in (1 cm) seam allowance.

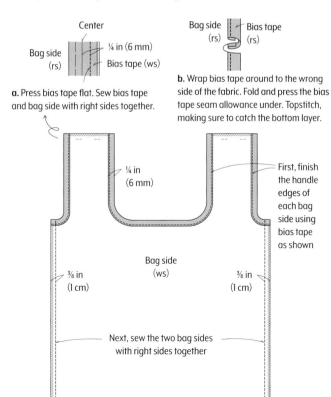

Center

Bag side (rs)

¼ in (6 mm)

Bias tape (ws)

a. Press bias tape flat. Sew bias tape and bag side with right sides together.

Bag side (rs)

Bias tape (rs)

b. Wrap bias tape around to the wrong side of the fabric. Fold and press the bias tape seam allowance under. Topstitch, making sure to catch the bottom layer.

¼ in (6 mm)

First, finish the handle edges of each bag side using bias tape as shown

⅜ in (1 cm)

Bag side (ws)

⅜ in (1 cm)

Next, sew the two bag sides with right sides together

3. With the wrong side of the bag facing out, fold the left and right edges in along the fold lines (refer to the template for placement). Using ⅜ in (1 cm) seam allowance, sew along the bottom of the bag, stitching the folds in place. Next, sew the folds in place on the handles using ⅜ in (1 cm) seam allowance.

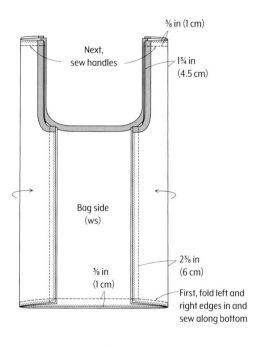

⅜ in (1 cm)

Next, sew handles

1¾ in (4.5 cm)

Bag side (ws)

⅜ in (1 cm)

2⅜ in (6 cm)

First, fold left and right edges in and sew along bottom

4. Turn the bag right side out. Use an iron to press the folds in place.

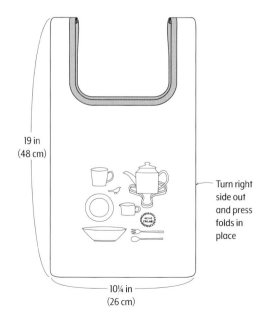

19 in (48 cm)

Turn right side out and press folds in place

10¼ in (26 cm)

Tobe Ware Sampler

SHOWN ON PAGES 36–37

MATERIALS

- DMC No. 25 embroidery floss in 322, 647, 676, and 988
- Linen thread in beige
- 12¾ × 15½ in (32 × 39 cm) of white linen fabric
- 11¾ × 14½ in (30 × 37 cm) of blue linen fabric
- 12¾ × 15½ in (32 × 39 cm) of mid-weight fusible interfacing
- 11¾ × 14½ in (30 × 37 cm) of paper-backed fusible web
- 9¼ × 11¼ in (23.5 × 28.5 cm) of ¼ in (5 mm) thick foam board
- Bookbinding tape

INSTRUCTIONS

1. Follow the instructions on page 61 to reverse appliqué the motif.
2. Embroider as noted in the diagram on page 107.
3. Once the embroidery is complete, fold the fabric around the foam board. Use bookbinding tape to secure the fabric in place on the wrong side of the foam board.

FINISHED SIZE

9¼ × 11¼ in (23.5 × 28.5 cm)

MOTIF (shown at 100%)

➤ Use 322 (2 strands) unless otherwise noted.

➤ Couching stitch around the outline of each appliqué motif using beige linen for main thread and 1 strand of No. 25 embroidery floss in 647 for the tacking thread.

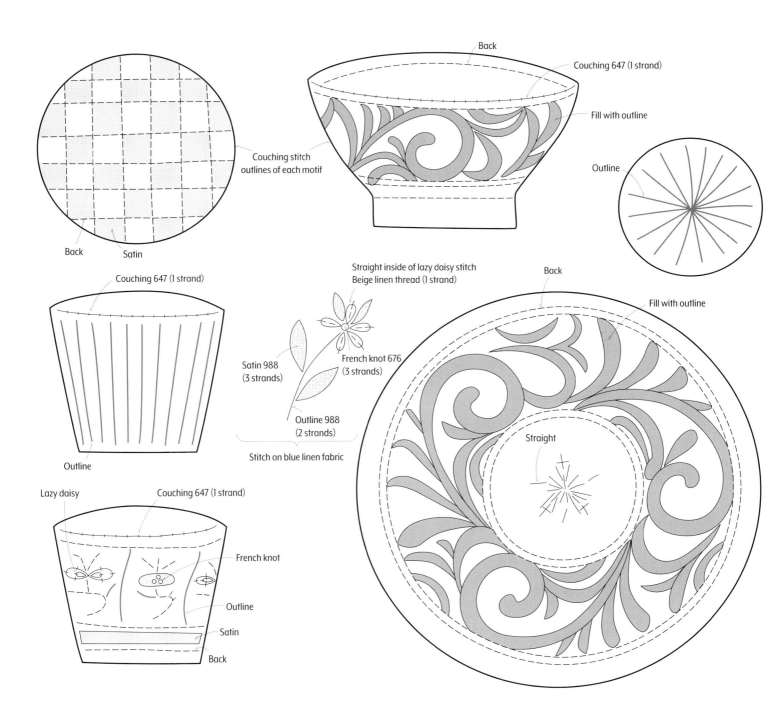

Back

Couching 647 (1 strand)

Fill with outline

Couching stitch outlines of each motif

Outline

Back   Satin

Couching 647 (1 strand)

Straight inside of lazy daisy stitch
Beige linen thread (1 strand)

Back

Fill with outline

Satin 988
(3 strands)

French knot 676
(3 strands)

Outline 988
(2 strands)

Stitch on blue linen fabric

Outline

Straight

Lazy daisy   Couching 647 (1 strand)

French knot

Outline

Satin

Back

Herb Patches

SHOWN ON PAGE 27

MATERIALS

→ DMC No. 25 embroidery floss in 320 and 368

→ 4 in (10 cm) square of white cotton sateen fabric

→ 4 in (10 cm) square of mid-weight fusible interfacing

→ Craft glue

INSTRUCTIONS

1. Adhere fusible interfacing to the wrong side of the white cotton sateen fabric.

2. Embroider the motifs as noted in the diagram below.

3. Use a toothpick to outline the motifs with craft glue, applying the glue to the white cotton sateen fabric about 1/16 in (2 mm) away from the embroidery.

4. Once the glue is dry, cut the motifs out just beyond the glue outline.

MOTIF (shown at 100%)

→ Use 3 strands unless otherwise noted.

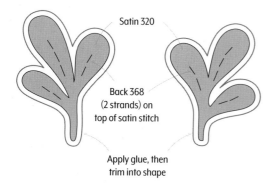

Satin 320

Back 368
(2 strands) on
top of satin stitch

Apply glue, then
trim into shape

Linen Bread Cloth

SHOWN ON PAGE 39

MATERIALS

→ DMC No. 25 embroidery floss in 347

→ One linen dish towel

→ Freezer paper

INSTRUCTIONS

1. Transfer the embroidery motif to the linen dish towel using the freezer paper method shown on page 60.

2. Embroider the motif as noted in the diagram below. If possible, hide your knots under the satin stitches on the right side of the towel.

3. Remove the freezer paper.

MOTIF (shown at 100%)

→ Use 347 for entire motif.

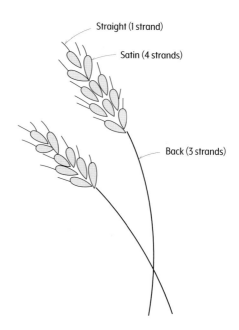

Straight (1 strand)

Satin (4 strands)

Back (3 strands)

Bread Magnets

SHOWN ON PAGE 38

MATERIALS

→ DMC No. 25 embroidery floss in ECRU, 433, 434, 435, 437, 738, 841, 3031, and 3865

→ 8 × 11¾ in (20 × 30 cm) of white linen fabric

→ 8 × 11¾ in (20 × 30 cm) of mid-weight fusible interfacing

→ Craft glue

INSTRUCTIONS

1. Adhere fusible interfacing to the wrong side of the white linen fabric.

2. Embroider the motifs as noted in the diagrams below.

3. Use a toothpick to outline the motifs with craft glue, applying the glue to the white linen fabric about ⅛ in (3 mm) away from the embroidery.

4. Once the glue is dry, cut the motifs out just beyond the glue outline.

MOTIFS (shown 100%)

→ Use 3 strands unless otherwise noted.

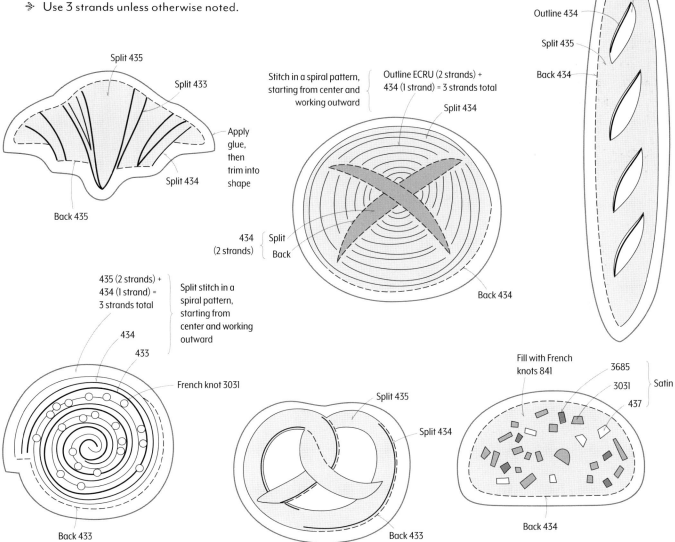

Recipe Case

SHOWN ON PAGE 40

MATERIALS

- DMC No. 25 embroidery floss in 304
- 9 × 13½ in (23 × 34 cm) of beige linen fabric (I used Libeco Napoli Vintage)
- 9 × 12¼ in (23 × 31 cm) of cotton fabric
- 2 in (5 cm) square of red leather
- One ¼ in (5 mm) eyelet
- 9¾ in (25 cm) of 1 mm thick leather cord
- Craft glue

INSTRUCTIONS

1. Cut a 9 × 13½ in (23 × 34 cm) rectangle of beige linen fabric for the pouch outside. Mark the finishing lines, as noted in the diagram below. Starting from the center, cross-stitch the front as noted in the diagram on page 111, stitching over two threads of the linen fabric to make each stitch. Use waste canvas if necessary.

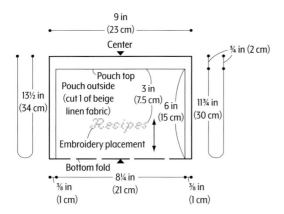

2. With right sides together, fold the pouch outside in half and sew along the sides using ⅜ in (1 cm) seam allowance. Align each side seam with the bottom fold and sew a ¾ in (2 cm) seam to miter the corners.

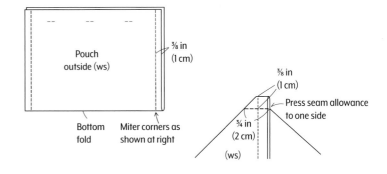

3. Cut a 9 × 12¼ in (23 × 31 cm) rectangle of cotton fabric for the pouch lining. Repeat step 2 to sew the lining.

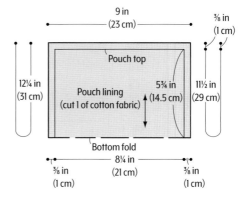

4. Turn the pouch outside right side out. Insert the lining into the pouch outside with wrong sides together. Fold and press the top seam allowances in so the lining is about ¼ in (5 mm) lower on the inside of the pouch. Hand stitch the lining in place on the inside of the pouch. Cut a 1⅛ in (2.8 cm) diameter leather circle and use an eyelet to attach it to the front of the pouch, as shown on page 64.

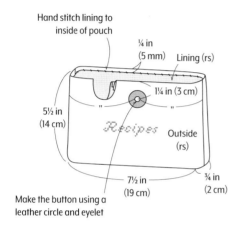

5. Knot the 9¾ in (25 cm) long leather cord at both ends. Cut a ¼ × ¾ in (0.5 × 2 cm) leather rectangle. Glue or sew the cord between the pouch back and leather rectangle as shown.

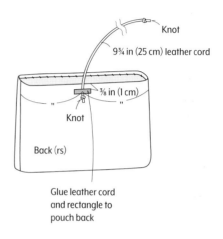

MOTIF

➢ Use 304 (2 strands) for entire motif.

➢ Each stitch should be made over two threads of the linen fabric.

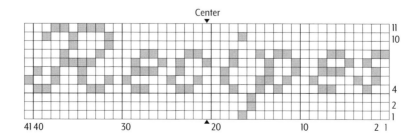

Monogrammed Oven Mitts

SHOWN ON PAGE 41

MATERIALS (FOR TWO OVEN MITTS)

- DMC No. 25 embroidery floss in 304
- 8 in (20 cm) square of beige linen fabric (I used Libeco Napoli Vintage)
- 8 in (20 cm) square of cotton fabric
- 8 in (20 cm) square of quilt batting
- Two ¼ × 3⅛ in (0.5 × 8 cm) pieces of red leather

INSTRUCTIONS

1. Use the template on page 113 to cut a semicircle of beige linen fabric for the outside (do not add seam allowance). Starting from the center, cross-stitch as noted in the diagrams on page 113, stitching over two threads of the linen fabric to make each stitch. Use waste canvas if necessary.

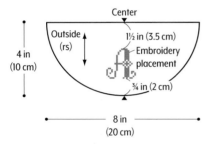

2. Use the template to cut a lining and piece of batting. Align the embroidered outside and lining with right sides together, then position the batting on top. Sew together around the curved edge using ¼ in (5 mm) seam allowance.

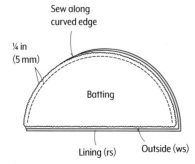

3. Pull the lining to separate it from the other layers, then fold to align the straight edges as shown. Fold the leather in half and pin in place between the two layers of outside fabric. Sew along the straight edges, leaving a 2 in (5 cm) opening in the lining.

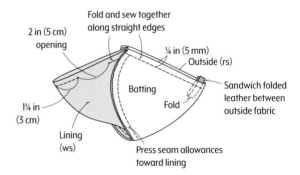

4. Turn right side out. Fold the seam allowances in and hand stitch the opening closed. Tuck the lining into the outside, then pull the lining down a bit so it is visible along the bottom of the oven mitt.

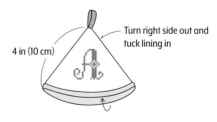

MOTIFS

↠ Use 304 (2 strands) for entire motif.

↠ Each stitch should be made over two threads of the linen fabric.

Customize with your own initials using these motifs as an example.

OVEN MITT TEMPLATE

Dala Horse Wall Hangings

SHOWN ON PAGES 48–49

MATERIALS (FOR ONE COLLAGE)

- DMC No. 25 embroidery floss in 336 (for A), 975 (for B), or 347 (for C), or floss that coordinates with your individual fabric
- 11 in (28 cm) square of beige linen fabric
- 7 in (18 cm) square of print fabric
- ¾ × 9¾ in (2 × 25 cm) fabric selvage
- 7 × 9¾ in (18 × 25 cm) of paper-backed fusible web
- 7 in (18 cm) square of ¼ in (5 mm) thick foam board
- Bookbinding tape
- 1¼ × 2 in (3 × 5 cm) piece of cardstock (for variation B)

FINISHED SIZE

7 in (18 cm) square

MOTIF (shown at 100%)

- Backstitch around the outline of the appliqué motif using 336 (for A), 975 (for B), or 347 (for C), or use floss that coordinates with your individual fabric

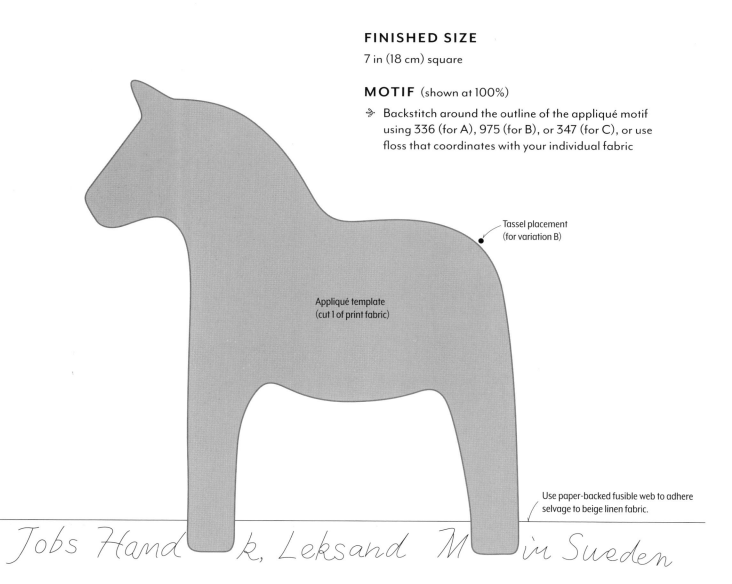

Tassel placement
(for variation B)

Appliqué template
(cut 1 of print fabric)

Use paper-backed fusible web to adhere
selvage to beige linen fabric.

Jobs Hand___k, Leksand M___ in Sweden

INSTRUCTIONS

1. Cut a ¾ × 9¾ in (2 × 25 cm) fabric selvage and use paper-backed fusible web to adhere it to the right side of the beige linen fabric (refer to the template on page 114 for placement).

2. Fussy cut the horse motif out of print fabric and appliqué to the beige linen fabric as shown in the guide on page 59. Backstitch around the outline of the appliqué motif as noted in the diagram on page 114.

3. For variation B, make a tassel for the tail as shown below and sew to the horse (refer to the template for placement).

4. Fold the fabric around the foam board. Use bookbinding tape to secure the fabric in place on the wrong side of the foam board.

How to Make a Tassel

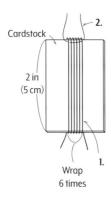

Cardstock

2.

2 in
(5 cm)

Wrap
6 times

1.

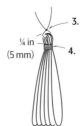

¼ in
(5 mm)

3.

4.

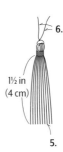

6.

1½ in
(4 cm)

5.

1. Wrap a piece of six-stranded embroidery floss around cardstock 6 times.

2. Loop a separate piece of floss through the wraps at the top.

3. Remove the cardstock. Tightly knot the floss looped through the top.

4. Use a separate piece of floss to wrap the tassel about ¼ in (5 mm) from the top. Knot the ends, then pull to hide the knot inside the tassel.

5. Cut the loops along the bottom and trim into shape.

6. Use the floss from step 2 to sew the tassel to the linen fabric.

Swedish Wildflower Sampler

SHOWN ON PAGE 50

MATERIALS

- DMC No. 25 embroidery floss in 320, 368, 646, 822, 989, 3820, and 3865
- DMC Pearl Cotton No. 5 in 368 and 989
- Linen thread in green, light green, buttercup yellow, lavender, and periwinkle blue
- 10¾ × 13¾ in (27 × 35 cm) of white linen fabric
- 10¾ × 13¾ in (27 × 35 cm) of mid-weight fusible interfacing
- 6¾ × 9¾ in (17 × 25 cm) of ¼ in (5 mm) thick foam board
- ¼ in (6 mm) wide light green organdy ribbon
- Invisible thread
- Bookbinding tape

INSTRUCTIONS

1. Adhere fusible interfacing to the wrong side of the white linen fabric.

2. Embroider as noted in the diagram on page 117.

3. Use the templates on page 117 to cut the light green organdy ribbon to size. Sew to the white linen fabric using invisible thread.

4. Fold the white linen fabric around the foam board. Use bookbinding tape to secure the fabric in place on the wrong side of the foam board.

FINISHED SIZE

6¾ × 9¾ in (17 × 25 cm)

MOTIF (shown on page 117)

- Use linen thread unless otherwise noted. When stitching with linen thread, use 1 strand unless otherwise noted

- #25 = No. 25 embroidery floss and #5 = Pearl Cotton No. 5. Unless otherwise noted, use 3 strands of No. 25 embroidery floss and 1 strand of Pearl Cotton No. 5.

MOTIF (shown at 100%)

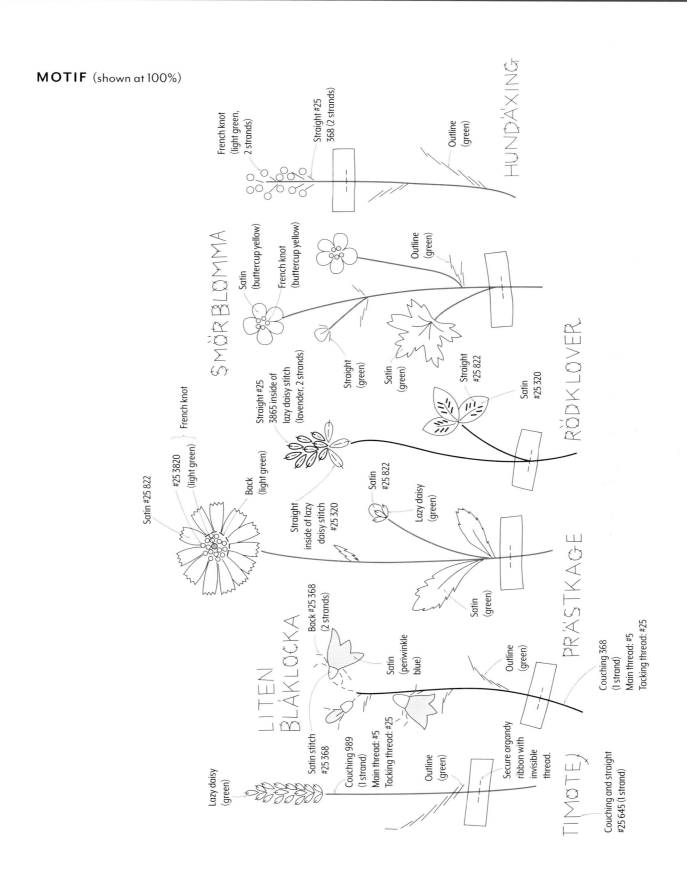

HUNDÄXING

French knot (light green, 2 strands)

Straight #25 368 (2 strands)

Outline (green)

SMÖR BLOMMA

Satin (buttercup yellow)

French knot (buttercup yellow)

Outline (green)

Straight (green)

Satin (green)

Straight #25 822

Satin #25 320

RÖDK LOVER

Straight #25 3865 inside of lazy daisy stitch (lavender, 2 strands)

French knot

Satin #25 822

#25 3820 (light green)

Back (light green)

Straight inside of lazy daisy stitch #25 320

Satin #25 822

Lazy daisy (green)

PRÄSTKAGE

Back #25 368 (2 strands)

Satin (periwinkle blue)

Outline (green)

Satin (green)

Couching 368 (1 strand)
Main thread: #5
Tacking thread: #25

LITEN BLÄKLOCKA

Satin stitch #25 368

Couching 989 (1 strand)
Main thread: #5
Tacking thread: #25

Outline (green)

Secure organdy ribbon with invisible thread.

TIMOTEJ

Lazy daisy (green)

Couching and straight #25 645 (1 strand)

Midsummer Tea Cozy

SHOWN ON PAGE 51

MATERIALS

- DMC No. 25 embroidery floss in ECRU, 316, 320, 435, 844, 3347, 3820, 3822, and 3865
- DMC Pearl Cotton No. 5 in 3347
- Linen thread in green, light green, and periwinkle blue
- 10¾ × 26 in (27 × 66 cm) of beige linen fabric
- 2 in (5 cm) square of white linen fabric
- 9 × 24¾ in (23 × 66 cm) of striped cotton fabric
- 8½ × 24½ in (21.5 × 62 cm) of fusible fleece
- 2 in (5 cm) square of mid-weight fusible interfacing
- Craft glue

INSTRUCTIONS

1. Embroider the beige linen fabric as noted in the diagram on Pattern Sheet B. Use the tea cozy outside template to trim the embroidered fabric into shape, then use the template to cut another tea cozy outside from the beige linen fabric. Next, use the proper template to cut two pieces of fusible fleece. Adhere the fusible fleece to the wrong side of the tea cozy outsides. Cut a 1¼ × 2¾ in (3 × 7 cm) rectangle of beige linen fabric for the loop.

2. Make the loop as shown in the diagram below. With right sides together, align the two tea cozy outsides with the folded loop sandwiched in between. Sew along the curved edge using ⅜ in (1 cm) seam allowance. Turn right side out.

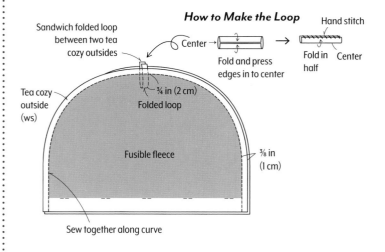

Diagram (left)

- 2¾ in (7 cm) — Loop
- 1¼ in (3 cm)
- ⅜ in (1 cm) seam allowance on tea cozy outsides only
- 8½ in (21.5 cm)
- Tea cozy outside (cut 2 of beige linen fabric and 2 of fusible fleece)
- Finishing line
- Bottom
- 10¾ in (27 cm)
- ¾ in (2 cm) seam allowance on tea cozy outsides only
- 13 in (33 cm)

How to Make the Loop

- Sandwich folded loop between two tea cozy outsides
- Center
- Fold and press edges in to center
- Hand stitch
- Fold in half
- Center
- Tea cozy outside (ws)
- ¾ in (2 cm)
- Folded loop
- Fusible fleece
- ⅜ in (1 cm)
- Sew together along curve

3. Use the template on Pattern Sheet B to cut two linings of striped cotton fabric. Align the two linings with right sides together and sew along the curved edge using ⅜ in (1 cm) seam allowance.

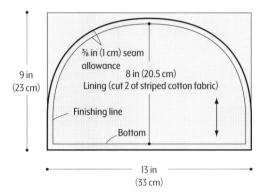

9 in (23 cm)

⅜ in (1 cm) seam allowance
8 in (20.5 cm)
Lining (cut 2 of striped cotton fabric)

Finishing line

Bottom

13 in (33 cm)

4. Insert the lining into the tea cozy with wrong sides together. Fold and press the bottom seam allowances in so about ⅜ in (1 cm) of the beige linen fabric is visible on the inside. Hand stitch the lining to the tea cozy on the inside. Make a few tacking stitches on the inside to attach the lining and outside at the top of the tea cozy. Make the butterfly as noted at right and sew to the tea cozy.

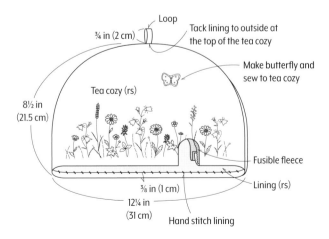

Loop
¾ in (2 cm)
Tack lining to outside at the top of the tea cozy

Tea cozy (rs)

Make butterfly and sew to tea cozy

8½ in (21.5 cm)

Fusible fleece

⅜ in (1 cm)
Lining (rs)

12¼ in (31 cm)
Hand stitch lining

How to Make the Butterfly

1. Adhere fusible interfacing to the wrong side of the white linen fabric.

2. Embroider the butterfly as noted in the diagram below.

3. Use a toothpick to outline the butterfly with craft glue, applying the glue to the white linen fabric about 1/16 in (2 mm) away from the embroidery.

4. Once the glue is dry, cut the motif out.

MOTIF (shown at 100%)

↝ Unless otherwise noted, use 3 strands of No. 25 embroidery floss.

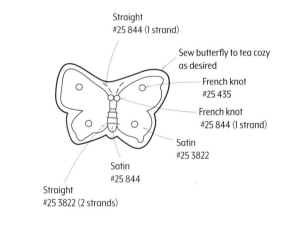

Straight
#25 844 (1 strand)

Sew butterfly to tea cozy as desired

French knot
#25 435

French knot
#25 844 (1 strand)

Satin
#25 3822

Satin
#25 844

Straight
#25 3822 (2 strands)

Sketchbook Studies

SHOWN ON PAGES 52–53

MATERIALS

For A

- → DMC No. 25 embroidery floss in 435, 610, 646, 727, 989, 3347, and 3821
- → DMC Pearl Cotton No. 5 in 989
- → ⅝ × 1 in (1.5 × 2.5 cm) of blue fabric
- → ⅝ × 1 in (1.5 × 2.5 cm) of paper-backed fusible web

For B

- → DMC No. 25 embroidery floss in 646 and 793

For C

- → DMC No. 25 embroidery floss in 347, 610, 646, and 3328

For Each

- → 4¾ × 7 in (12 × 18 cm) of white linen fabric
- → 4¾ × 7 in (12 × 18 cm) of mid-weight fusible interfacing

INSTRUCTIONS

1. Adhere fusible interfacing to the wrong side of the white linen fabric.

2. For variation A only, use paper-backed fusible web to adhere the blue fabric to the white linen fabric (refer to the diagram at right for placement).

3. Embroider the motifs as noted in the diagrams at right and on page 121.

4. Trim the white linen fabric to 4¾ × 7 in (12 × 18 cm). Use a hole punch and scissors along the top to recreate the look of a page torn from a notebook.

FINISHED SIZE

4¾ × 7 in (12 × 18 cm)

MOTIF A (shown at 100%)

- → Use 3 strands unless otherwise noted.
- → #25 = No. 25 embroidery floss and #5 = Pearl Cotton No. 5.

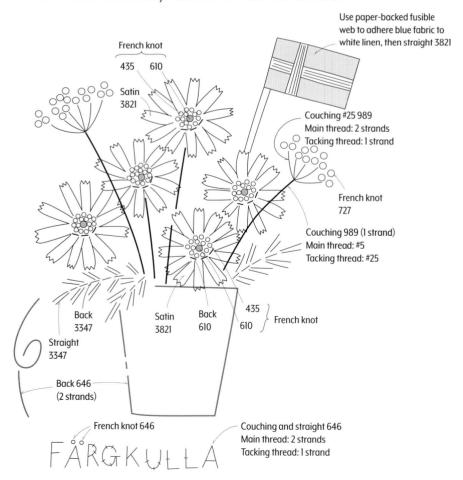

French knot
435   610

Satin
3821

Use paper-backed fusible web to adhere blue fabric to white linen, then straight 3821

Couching #25 989
Main thread: 2 strands
Tacking thread: 1 strand

French knot
727

Couching 989 (1 strand)
Main thread: #5
Tacking thread: #25

Back
3347

Satin
3821

Back
610

435
610   French knot

Straight
3347

Back 646
(2 strands)

French knot 646

Couching and straight 646
Main thread: 2 strands
Tacking thread: 1 strand

FÄRGKULLA

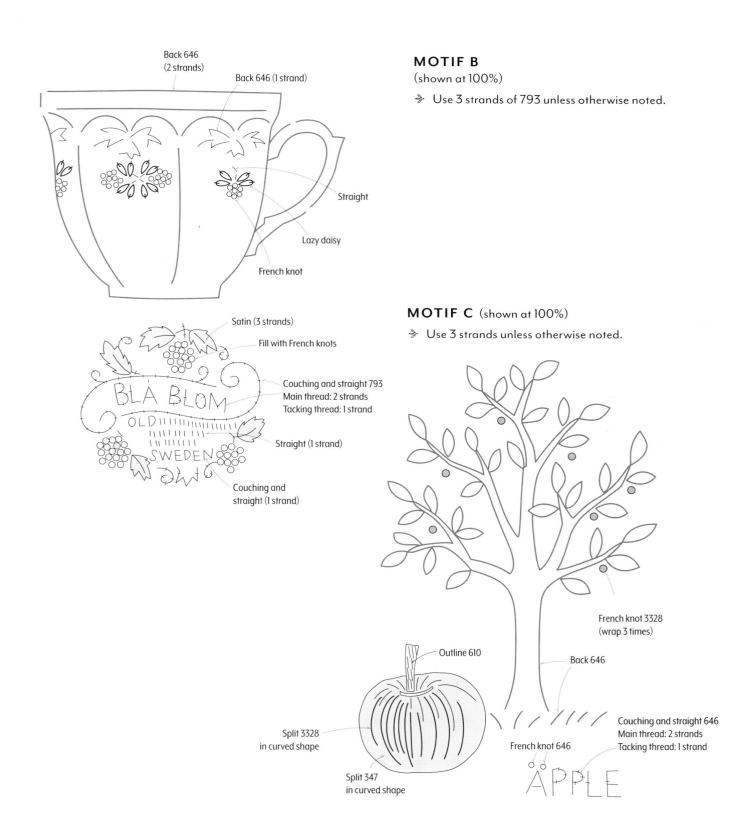

Back 646
(2 strands)

Back 646 (1 strand)

MOTIF B
(shown at 100%)

⇢ Use 3 strands of 793 unless otherwise noted.

Straight

Lazy daisy

French knot

Satin (3 strands)

Fill with French knots

Couching and straight 793
Main thread: 2 strands
Tacking thread: 1 strand

Straight (1 strand)

Couching and
straight (1 strand)

BLÅ BLOM
OLD
SWEDEN

MOTIF C (shown at 100%)

⇢ Use 3 strands unless otherwise noted.

French knot 3328
(wrap 3 times)

Outline 610

Back 646

Split 3328
in curved shape

Split 347
in curved shape

French knot 646

Couching and straight 646
Main thread: 2 strands
Tacking thread: 1 strand

APPLE

Mushroom Needlebook

SHOWN ON PAGE 54

MATERIALS

- ↣ DMC No. 25 embroidery floss in ECRU, 347, 349, 433, and 3865
- ↣ 4 × 7 in (10 × 18 cm) of beige linen fabric
- ↣ 6¼ in (16 cm) square of ivory felt
- ↣ 3¼ × 6¼ in (8 × 16 cm) of mid-weight fusible interfacing
- ↣ 14 in (36 cm) of ⅛ in (4 mm) wide linen ribbon
- ↣ Alphabet rubber stamps
- ↣ Sepia ink pad (suitable for use on fabric)

INSTRUCTIONS

1. Cut a 4 × 7 in (10 × 18 cm) rectangle of beige linen fabric and a 3¼ × 6¼ in (8 × 16 cm) rectangle of fusible interfacing. Mark the finishing lines on the wrong side of the beige linen fabric and adhere fusible interfacing. Stamp and embroider the motif as noted in the diagram on page 123.

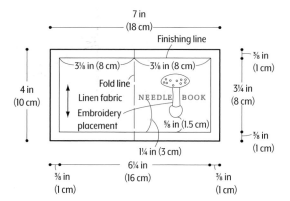

2. Mark the finishing lines on the right side of the beige fabric, then backstitch as noted below. To miter the corners, first measure ⅜ in (1 cm) from each corner and mark. Connect adjacent marks with a diagonal line. Cut along the diagonal lines to trim the corners. Next, fold each corner so the crease intersects with the finishing line corner point. Finally, fold each side in along the marked finishing lines to complete the miter.

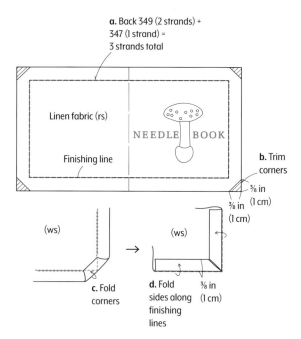

3. Cut two 3¼ × 6¼ in (8 × 16 cm) rectangles of ivory felt.

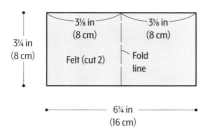

4. Layer the two pieces of felt. Fold in half at the center to crease. Running stitch along the crease to create the book's pages.

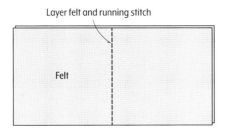

5. Hand stitch the bottom layer of felt to the wrong side of the linen fabric along the bottom. Next, tack two 7 in (18 cm) pieces of linen ribbon to the wrong side of the linen fabric along the sides, then continue hand stitching the bottom layer of felt in place along the other three edges.

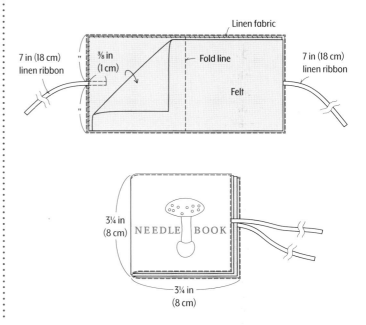

MOTIF (shown at 100%)

→ Use 3 strands unless otherwise noted.

→ Refer to pin cushion motif on page 125 for embroidery instructions.

Mushroom Pin Cushion

SHOWN ON PAGE 54

MATERIALS

- ⤳ DMC No. 25 embroidery floss in ECRU, 347, 349, 433, and 3865
- ⤳ 4¾ × 8 in (12 × 20 cm) of beige linen fabric
- ⤳ 15¾ in (40 cm) of ⅜ in (8 mm) wide linen ribbon
- ⤳ Stuffing

- ⤳ Brass squirrel charm
- ⤳ Alphabet rubber stamps
- ⤳ Sepia ink pad (suitable for use on fabric)

INSTRUCTIONS

1. Stamp and embroider the beige linen fabric as noted in the diagram on page 125. Sew the squirrel charm in place.

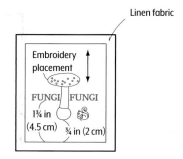

2. Trim the embroidered fabric into a 4 × 4¾ in (10 × 12 cm) rectangle, then cut an equally sized rectangle for the back.

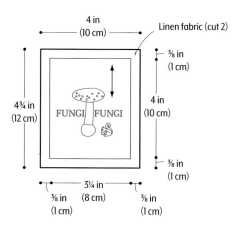

3. Align the two rectangles with right sides together. Use ⅜ in (1 cm) seam allowance to sew around all four sides, leaving a 1½ in (4 cm) opening.

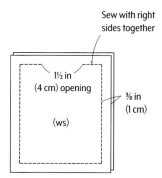

4. Turn right side out. Fill with stuffing, then fold the seam allowances in and hand stitch the opening closed.

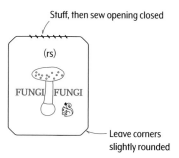

5. Hand stitch the linen ribbon to the seam as shown below.

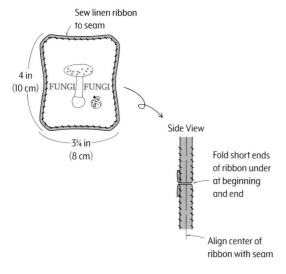

Sew linen ribbon to seam

4 in (10 cm)

FUNGI FUNGI

3¼ in (8 cm)

Side View

Fold short ends of ribbon under at beginning and end

Align center of ribbon with seam

MOTIF (shown at 100%)

↬ Use 3 strands unless otherwise noted.

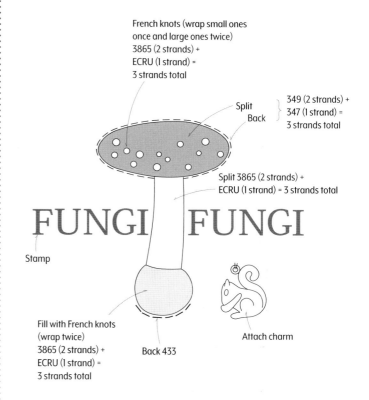

French knots (wrap small ones once and large ones twice)
3865 (2 strands) +
ECRU (1 strand) =
3 strands total

Split
Back

349 (2 strands) +
347 (1 strand) =
3 strands total

Split 3865 (2 strands) +
ECRU (1 strand) = 3 strands total

FUNGI FUNGI

Stamp

Fill with French knots (wrap twice)
3865 (2 strands) +
ECRU (1 strand) =
3 strands total

Back 433

Attach charm

Embroidery Stitch Guide

Straight Stitch

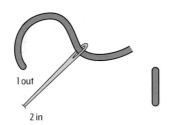

Running Stitch

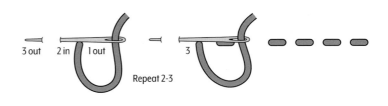

Couching Stitch

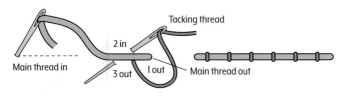

Make small straight stitches with tacking thread to secure the main thread.

Backstitch

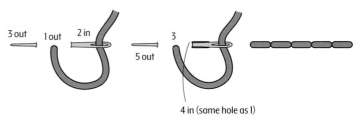

Outline Stitch

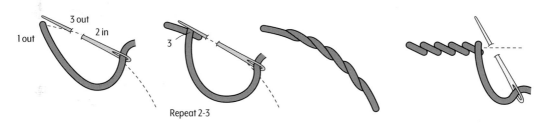

For a thicker line, increase the overlapped portions of the stitches.

Fill with Outline Stitch

Fill with outline stitch following the shape of the motif.

Split Stitch

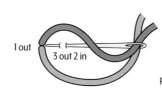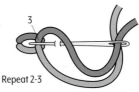

This stitch is worked just like outline stitch, but you'll actually bring the needle back up through the middle of each stitch, splitting the fibers apart.

Buttonhole Stitch (open)

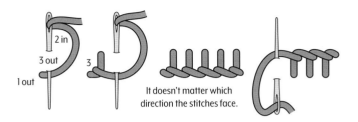

It doesn't matter which direction the stitches face.

Buttonhole Stitch (closed)

Use the same process as the open buttonhole stitch, but make the stitches as close together as possible.

French Knot (wrap once)

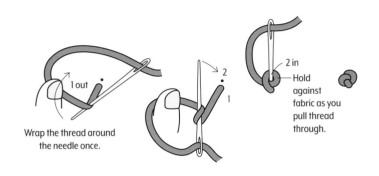

Wrap the thread around the needle once.

Hold against fabric as you pull thread through.

Fill with French Knots

Make French knots close together to fill an area.

French Knot (wrap twice)

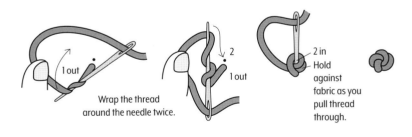

Wrap the thread around the needle twice.

Hold against fabric as you pull thread through.

Satin Stitch

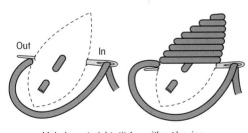

Make long straight stitches without leaving any space between stitches.

Long and Short Stitch

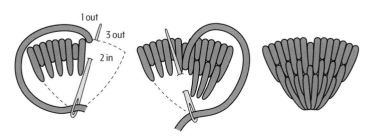

Fill an area with straight stitches of varying lengths.

Satin Stitch with Core

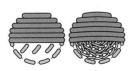

For added thickness, fill the outline with straight or chain stitches, then work the satin stitch on top.

Chain Stitch

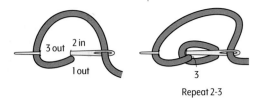

3 out
2 in
1 out

3

Repeat 2-3

Lazy Daisy Stitch

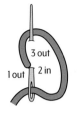

4 in

3 out
1 out
2 in

Bullion Knot

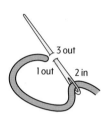
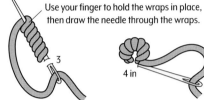

3 out
1 out
2 in

Use your finger to hold the wraps in place, then draw the needle through the wraps.

3

4 in

Fly Stitch

1 out
2 in
3 out

3

4 in

Spider Web Rose

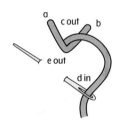
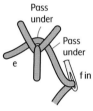
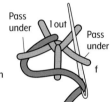

a
c out
b
e out
d in

Pass under
Pass under
e
f in

Pass under
1 out
Pass under
f

2 in

Stitch five spokes. Draw the thread out. Weave the thread under and over the spokes in a spiral pattern to fill the wheel. Insert the thread back through the fabric to finish.

Needleweaving Stitch

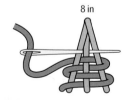

2, 4, and 6 in

3 out   1 out   5 out

7 out

8 in

Weave the thread between the vertical stitches, working from left to right, then right to left alternately.

Cross-Stitch

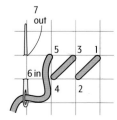
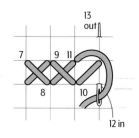
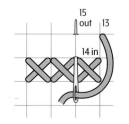
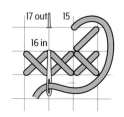

7 out
5   3   1
6 in
4   2

13 out
7   9 11
8   10
12 in

15 out 13
14 in

17 out 15
16 in